Featuring Heartfelt Stories
and Practical Wisdom

To Louise
Love Trish Jones.
x

Refined by Fire

D1806511

Defining Moments of
Phenomenal Women

Compiled by Anthony and Crystal Obey

www.GMApublishing.com
www.RefinedbyFireWomen.com

Printed in the United States of America.

All Scripture taken from NIV unless otherwise noted.

Books in the Refined by Fire Series
Finding Purpose in Your Pain
Discovering Victory through Adversity
Secrets of Becoming a Champion of Life Challenges
Defining Moments of Phenomenal Women

TABLE OF
CONTENTS
ॐ◌ल

INTRODUCTION

There are women all over the world at this very moment who have gone through, are going through, and will go through fiery trials that threaten their faith and everything they value. Being driven to the edge of reason is an experience that marks the soul of many women of faith at one time or another.

Where do women go when the heat's on?

What provisions has God made for the needs of His daughters?

Where does one find healing and restoration for the pain that they've experienced?

What forum provides laughter and entertainment while delivering inspiration and insight?

Among the greatest of tools that God has provided for a woman's healing and encouragement is the *Refined by Fire* book series. God ensures us that in moments of this life, we will suffer. He warns us of this because He wants us to know that the fires that surprisingly break out in our lives are not news to Him. He knows the pain that each one of us will endure in life. He's not naïve nor does He want us to be ignorant of the fact that though we are chosen for a purpose, we will endure some pain and shed a few tears. But be encouraged because all of these things work together to transform us into phenomenal vessels of honor.

God desires to dwell with us and bless us richly in all areas of our lives. He makes His bountiful inheritance available to us even at this moment, but we must continually mature in order to be found worthy of dwelling in greater dimensions of this inheritance.

Consider the beautiful butterfly. Not a single one of them have received their wings without a struggle. One would think that a butterfly was born being the lovely creatures they are. We would never imagine that a butterfly would *struggle* in order to develop the wings that make them so precious. But on the contrary, it is the very *process* of struggling to set its self free from the shadow of its former existence that defines the beautiful wings of this creature.

As a matter of fact, without the struggling process of the young butterfly breaking through the ugly shell called its *cocoon*, the butterfly will never develop her beautiful wings, nor will she grace the fields with her prancing flight.

Like the butterfly, God uses the process of life to make us beautifully mature in time. You will discover as you read this book that the process is priceless! The good times as well as the bad times all work together to shape and mold us into vessels worthy to reign with the Father of Creation for all eternity. Our Father often allows us to struggle in our attempts to break free from the cocoons of our past in order to strengthen our faith, love, and devotion to Him. This is the path of truly phenomenal women.

In this book, *Refined by Fire: Defining Moments of Phenomenal Women*, women share some of the most critical moments of their lives. These are moments that tested every fiber of their being. These moments are those that easily break some, but these women reveal their secret treasury of tenacity, faith, and resilience in the midst of a crisis.

Some of these moments are tragic while some are miraculous. Some of the moments will make you laugh while others will make you cry. Some of them will challenge you to grow while still others will confirm your faith.

Each story may invoke different emotions in you but there are a few things that are guaranteed to those who read *Defining Moments of Phenomenal Women*.

You will gain new insight into God's heart and love for you.

You will be empowered to do the right thing even if you have to take a loss.

You will be comforted, knowing that you're not alone in your pain and struggles.

You will be healed by being able to relate to other women who have felt some of the same pains you have felt and thought some of the same doubtful thoughts you are thinking, and have crossed some of the same crossroads that you have yet to cross.

When you expect a change to come in life and it doesn't come, you can reflect on the experiences of these women to find the solace and peace you need to wait on God.

This book series is based on the powerful scripture: *That the genuineness of your faith, being much more precious than gold that perishes, though it is refined by fire, may be found to praise, honor, and glory at the revelation of Jesus Christ* (1 Peter 1: 7).

We present to you the life and times of women of faith. Snuggle up with a soothing cup of cocoa in your favorite spot and enjoy this special collection of defining moments shared by phenomenal women.

THOMASINE PICKENS

If I Knew Then What I Know Now

It was an unbearably long season of my life. Everything that I touched seemed to tarnish right before my eyes, beginning with the mysterious deaths of my parents. My father fell into a lake while fishing with my nephew and my mother. Then almost two years later, my mother, 51, suffered a sudden heart attack and died. I had a close relative tell me, "If it wasn't for bad luck you would have no luck at all!"

In the midst of all of this I married a man that did not love me. He vowed that he would never hit me but he would verbally abuse me and he did so often throughout our eight and a half years of marriage. He would go days and sometimes weeks without even speaking or looking at me. All of this brought so much confusion and pain; but I did not know how to make the pain stop.

The birth of my son gave me a reason to live. I tried to focus on being a mother but many times felt that I was not doing a very good job.

Many Christians continued to tell me to "get over" the loss of my parents and move on with my life. I was unable to because of the abuse that I was receiving from my husband.

I couldn't understand why God would "take" my parents during the years that I felt I needed them the most. I asked God if He even liked me. I felt that God was laughing at all of my pain and frustration. I wondered why God allowed me to marry a man who displayed such a dislike for me. I began to make bad choices and do things that were not of God—trying to fill my emptiness, my void.

My son and I moved to a new city while my husband was stationed overseas and were involved in a terrible car accident. My son wasn't even one year of age when he was thrown from the car. He was sitting in my lap because his car seat was in my car that was at the shop. My son was tossed from the vehicle and was flipping in midair while cars were crashing all around him. My son did not receive a scratch! I was sore and bruised, but no broken bones. The vehicles involved in the accident were totaled but we walked away with our lives.

Though I was thankful my son was healthy, I again questioned God as to why He let this happen. My husband and I were discussing divorce because there was no love in the marriage. I was hurting and he was hurting me more by continuing to reject me.

I did not think I could support myself and a baby, so I talked him into staying with me. I wasn't happy, but I was waiting on my miracle from God. I felt that if I could just hold on God would eventually stop being angry with me and begin to love me. I felt that I had no one to turn to who could understand my problems, so I turned to alcohol. I began to drink every day.

I was not able to maintain friendships due to my own issues. I would push people away by being rude to them. I wasn't close to any of my family members during this season of my life. It seemed that everyone was able to function and I was the only dysfunctional one. I fought depression. I wanted God to just stop being so horrible to me and just take my life!

My marriage was at its very worst when I started having affairs…still trying to fill my void. I felt that if my husband did not want to be with me I would find someone else to be with me. I had the mindset of "just give me what I want and go." I was now fighting a very ugly lustful and adulterous spirit. My husband did not care what I did, just as long as I did not bother him. He never questioned my outings and did not care when I returned.

> **I felt that my husband would love me if I did everything right.**

When my husband got out of the military I felt assured that he would be a better husband and father. So I decided that I would change my life and become a better mother and wife. I felt that my husband would love me if I did everything right. I wanted to be married because I did not want to be a single parent-I still did not think I could take care of my son and myself.

After finding a church, I finally began to deal with all of my issues (the pain, the hurt, the rejection that I felt so deep within my heart). When I became pregnant again, I felt that a second child would complete our marriage and family life. My husband started going to church. However, it

8

ended after the birth of our second son. My husband was still blessed with a very good paying job. The mental abuse started up again and I began to have an affair again.

I felt a strong desire for my family, including my husband, to move to Texas with my grandmother and aunt. But my husband declined the move, so we stayed. In February of 1994, seven months after the birth of our second son, my husband packed up his bags and moved out while I was at work.

Why would God allow him to leave me with two children, no education, and no way to take care of my children? I had no choice but to start my new life alone with my children. I was there with two babies (age 5 years and 7 months), no mother, no father, and no husband.

Although we were not in love with one another my husband was my security blanket. I had finally learned how to ignore the mental abuse. I truly thought this storm would destroy me. Here I was 27 years old, single, no college education and two children. I was not making enough money to take care of my sons.

I met a wonderful man who gave me everything my husband did not give me—love and attention. I thought we would be together forever. I was finally happy after all of those years. I had my dream man and soon to be husband as well as my sons. God had finally answered my prayers and I truly thought God now loved me.

Within three months of this relationship, I found out that my dream man had some drug issues; and though I was willing to work with him, he too left me. I was now pregnant with my third child and alone.

God, what are you doing to me? Why was it so hard for me to find love? I searched and I searched for my dream man and to no avail. Every man I met was a taker not a giver. In the end, I lost my apartment, I lost all of my possessions that were in storage and my babies and I were "homeless" with nothing but a few clothes. At this point, I was feeling stupid and ashamed.

I was 30 years of age, divorced, no money, three sons (ages 7, 2 and a newborn) and all alone. I found myself living in an old house in a rough area that was falling apart and had rats because my credit was bad due to my divorce and inability to pay my bills.

At Church, I was constantly asked to go to a room with hundreds of talking babies and their parents. I began to stay home and watch church on TV; yearning to be there, but unable to do so because of my young children. Now I was really angry with God.

I was outside during a rain storm one day, crying in the middle of the street and I asked God, "Where are You?!" I reminded the Lord that I had given my life to Him at the tender age of 12. As a young teenager I always knew that I was to serve the Lord. I did not have any idea what that meant, but I wanted to do it.

I began to scream and stomp in the middle of the street. "God, where are YOU? What is my purpose? If I don't have one, then please take me home. I don't want to do this life thing anymore. I'm tired…I'm sick of life! I've failed in everyway possible. I'm lonely and I want a husband. I want my family to be complete."

Finally I heard an audible voice say "I'm right here waiting for you." I suddenly stopped in the middle of my tantrum. I could not believe God had spoken to me. He said it again, "I'm right here waiting for you."

The Lord told me to follow Him. He told me to pack up and move to San Antonio, Texas to fulfill my purpose.

I did not have any money and had no job or a place to stay in San Antonio. A few days later I received a call from my aunt that my grandmother was aging and she needed some assistance. She said the Lord told her to call me to see if I would move there and help her. My aunt had just moved my grandmother into her home. The rent at my grandmother's apartment was paid for the year and I was approved to stay there.

My life changed as I packed up our things and placed my sons in the backseat of our car and started our journey to find purpose. As we arrived in San Antonio, we settled into a two bedroom, two bathroom furnished apartment! The following Sunday we went to church and I rededicated my life to Jesus Christ. I was welcomed into the Body of Christ and immediately I began to see my purpose in life. For the very first time in my adult life, I had peace! I felt safe, I felt loved, I felt understood and I felt like God really did love me.

At a single's conference, I was introduced to my spiritual Husband—Jesus Christ, the lover of my soul! I had never felt the presence of the Lord on that level. I received deliverance and I knew that my life would never be the same!

Finally, the void in my spirit was filled! The Lord again spoke to me through Jeremiah 1:17. He continued to tell me that He had created me to be an Evangelist and teach His Word. I must laugh at myself because I had no idea what an evangelist was at the time. I contacted my aunt so she could explain to me the job duties of an evangelist. I went back to my living room and asked the Lord if He would "please give me another assignment because I was not qualified." I struggled with my assignment, but I agreed to do whatever God needed me to do.

I had a hard time dealing with Friday nights because in my mind that was date night with your man. I would take my sons to the movies to only sit there and cry while I saw husbands and wives, boyfriends and girlfriends together holding hands and laughing. My heart wept for I truly desired a husband.

My first assignment was to have a Friday night bible study in my home with two other women and their children. The ladies and I would cook dinner together and enjoy a long evening of the Word of God. My next assignments included starting a Singles Ministry and attending Seminary.

The Lord had me to start another women's bible study group in my home with women from outside the church. The Lord took the Virtuous Women Bible Study group, *T Pickens Ministry* and birthed the church, *Real Word Ministries Inc.* from it. The church opened on Sunday, June 6, 2004 in San Antonio, Texas. I am the Co-Pastor and Jesus is the Pastor.

I am now 41 years of age with my three sons that I raised by myself in the natural and with my Heavenly Father and spiritual husband. My sons are now ages 18, 13, and 11. The Lord has still not sent me a husband in the natural. I enjoy preaching His Word to people who are lost and feel unloved to give them Hope in the midst of their storms. The Lord gave me *Real 2 Reel*, which means you must be real about your struggles in order to reel in the people for Jesus.

If I knew then what I know now, I would have never taken my eyes off of Jesus Christ. I thank God for all of my struggles, hard times, and sad days. Psalm 37:4 says "Trust in the Lord and do good; dwell in the land and enjoy safe pasture. Delight yourself in the Lord and he will give you the desires of your heart." You see, I had placed all of my trust in a man. I was expecting a man to make me happy and to take care of me. A play was birthed from this entitled "Sugar Daddy." I want to show women how to let go of their natural *sugar daddy* and be embraced by their Spiritual Sugar Daddy.

I am no longer angry at God. I know that I'm one of His favorite daughters. Being a divorced, female, African-American Pastor has its challenges, but I know the plan for my life!

My life is truly perfect because of Jesus! He has loved me and continues to bless me beyond my wildest dreams. He has proven Himself faithful to us. We have since left the apartment, bought a townhouse and we now reside in a two story beautiful home in a new neighborhood. I have since owned four new cars in my name only! God did it!!! He gives me everything that I ask for and He provides every single need that my sons and I may have.

❧2❧

VALARIE FISH

The Castaway

The water is cold. The surge pushes me up and for a few seconds I can see all the way to the horizon. Then I ride the wave back down, water surrounding me on every side. Up and down with the billows, I strain in every direction looking for something to hold on to, something to keep me afloat.

How long can I tread water?

I know how I came to be here. The labor pains were intense but the doctor said I wasn't dilating. They gave me something in my IV to increase the intensity of the contractions. During one vicious contraction I felt something pop in my abdomen.

"A pop?" the Doctor seemed perplexed.

"I really can't describe it any other way. It felt like a pop."

The monitor with its long flat tongue spat out more readings. The baby's heart rate slowed.

The nurses roll me to one side; pain so intense I can't help but cry out. No change. "Try rolling to the other side." The pain is searing through my stomach.

Something's wrong. Can't you see that something is wrong?

"Prep for surgery." The doctor barks orders even as he tries to remain calm. "The baby is in distress but we can't find a reason for it. We need to do a C-section."

I'm too far gone to respond.

"Doctor, we've lost the heartbeat."

So here I am, dumped without warning into this endless expanse. I begin to fall the moment the doctor stands over me in the recovery room to explain the ruptured uterus and how my perfect baby boy died before they could get to him.

Instinct tells me I must survive while a small part of me wonders if I really want to continue to tread water. Of course I must survive. I have a husband and one son already who need me. Besides, all things work together for good, right?

I may just slap the next person that tells me that.

The graveside service is over and the mailbox continues to spew condolences from churches and individuals. Some are friends and some know us through our ministry. Each kind word provides a little strength to keep me treading.

Eventually all the cards are read and they stop coming. Now what am I going to hold on to?

As a preacher's wife, preacher's daughter, and preacher's granddaughter, I have church work and Christian service in my DNA. Apart from bouts of teenage rebellion I have served faithfully for many years. Choir, Sunday school, church camp, Vacation Bible school, fundraisers and benefits – all are important and an integral part of my life. I even work in a church-sponsored home for abused and neglected children. I'm a professional mom. Who better to have a new baby?

> *I suppose this is what some call a defining moment, the point in time that changes one's perspective on every aspect of life.*

Why is God doing this to me?

I suppose this is what some call a defining moment, the point in time that changes one's perspective on every aspect of life. As I tread water I must examine what I might have within me to help me stay afloat.

My faith is predictable and my religion comfortable – until now.

God, I have done everything I'm supposed to do. This should be an "I'll scratch Your back, You scratch mine" kind of deal.

Still He is silent and the waves are growing. I'm tired.

Just tell me what to do.

The local grief support group sits in a circle and each one talks about his or her loved one. An elderly man is grieving the loss of his bride of almost 50 years. Another woman has recurring nightmares about where the police may find the body of her daughter, missing for over two years. My own pain seems small in contrast.

Can't somebody help me?

The Bible stories are familiar but not applicable. I've taught them all to various age groups complete with flannel graph and coloring sheets.

13

They are just stories, and yet my upbringing tells me that every answer I need can be found in the Word.

Who in the Bible has been where I am? Whom can I look to for advice? Who has found himself treading water and wondering if rescue is in sight?

Two men come readily to mind—Job, who lost everything, and David, who mourned the death of a son.

What does Job know that I don't know? I take the time to read his story again, maybe even for the first time. Not many coloring sheets with Job's story. He didn't know why he was treading water. His wife wanted him to give up, but he kept kicking. Job didn't focus on getting explanations concerning his circumstances, but rather he took inventory of what he knew to be true.

The Lord gives and the Lord takes away (Job 1:21). With bitter tears I acknowledged His right to take my baby. I don't like it and I still want to know why.

I know that my Redeemer lives (Job 19:25) and that He has a purpose for every step that I take (Job 23:10). Can God think I am going to be content with the fact that my baby is waiting for me in heaven and that this loss was all part of some grand plan? I don't think I'm ready for that.

I moved on to see how David coped with the death of his son. David lost his son because of sin in his life. I relate better with Job. No adultery or murder in my history. Still David appeals to me because he has such poetry to his prayers. How did he do that? How did he find something to pull him up out of the violent waves?

"My sin is always before me" (Psalm 51:3b).

As I said, no major sin in my life.

Except pride,

And self-righteousness,

And religion instead of a relationship.

I gag as I swallow a mouthful of bitter truth. Is this what I needed to be able to see my own hollowness? Couldn't there have been some other way?

Confession is slow to come but when it finally takes hold the floodgates open.

Father, I have accepted Your sacrifice but I haven't loved You for it. I have served you because of Your sacrifice and I have thanked You for my salvation but I haven't loved You. I want to love You.

"Before I was afflicted I went astray; but now I have kept your word" (Psalm 119:67).

14

All my life I have taught the stories of the Bible to others, usually based on a storehouse of information from my own childhood. No fresh words only stale leftovers. How could I have been content with such fare? Worse yet, how could I have thought that God would be satisfied with my serving such a meal to others? Not only satisfied but even impressed?

Slowly I dedicate myself to devouring the Word like a starving castaway. The Word becomes my life preserver, and as I begin to fall in love with Him I notice that the waves are calming and a sandy shoal is beneath my feet. I have not even noticed an oasis rising up from the deepest abyss.

Standing now with the humble realization that only through the hopelessness of the waves have I found the only solid foundation to stand on, I turn to see others like me – floundering in the depths, unable to see the life preservers in the Word.

Can they hear me if I shout?

"I've been where you are, Sister!"

"There is hope. Don't stop treading!"

Now that my strength is renewed, maybe I can reach them. I will carry my own preserver with me and maybe they will find what I have found. I know that "If his Word had not been my delight, I would have perished in my affliction" (Psalm 119:92).

Sitting in a wheelchair next to the smallest coffin I had ever seen I held a pillow tightly to my physical scars as I sobbed. One exquisite hand held a stuffed Eeyore, a newly crocheted afghan tucked lovingly around his flawless body.

This would be a defining moment in a journey I was destined to make. A journey that I would not ask God to remove from me because it has taken me to a place of sweet surrender that I might not have found any other way.

I may face another journey in my future and I may find myself in another sea of despair. As difficult as it is to say, I know for certain as Job did (23:10) – "He knows the way that I take and when He has tried me I will come forth as gold."

❧3❧

TAMMIE JUDD

Pressed Down but Not Destroyed!

I didn't wake up angry that morning two years ago. I had actually woken up with praise in my heart. All was right with the world. Then my feet hit the floor. My leg muscles were weak—my balance a little off. "I'll wake up," I told myself.

My girlfriend and I attended a ministry conference for four days in Chicago. We were pampered and treated wonderfully. The ministry that paid for us to come really made us feel loved; providing both of us with private rooms we wouldn't be able to afford on our own.

It was there at that conference, in one of my private times with God, sitting on an old log in the middle of a wooded area, I committed to God to heed to the call He had put into my heart. I realized that for four years I had been resting in His shadow.

Sure, I was still in full-time ministry as a junior/senior high school teacher; however, four years ago, I was working at a ministry in a Federal Prison, a director for a Christian Learning Center, and involved in most of the ministries at our church. There was never any down time. God had blessed me with the most patient, loving husband anyone could pray for; and, our five children truly are gifts from above. However, time was snatched from me, and time with them was very scarce. Somehow in striving to *please* God, I had allowed Satan to seduce me with the ministries in which others would not work. Satan has a way of shaming you into taking a ministry that was never yours to have. He has a way of sounding so much like God, yet there is never real peace. I looked around at my life at that point. I felt pulled in all directions. I didn't understand how it could be *bad*—after all, I was encouraging the saints, helping the sick, visiting the widows, ministering to the poor, giving hope to women in prison…but there was sadness.

"There must be something more to this life," I thought. "More than the hustle and bustle of everything." It finally hit me when I was laughingly called the *invisible mom!* The children could see evidence I was there—the love notes, the packed lunches, the hot meals…but the visible mom was always busy…even if she was home.

I lived by lists and time schedules. I felt suffocated by life. Something had to change. I was crying out to God. "HELP ME, LORD!" I cried. It didn't take long until He took the blinders off. The true test of everything—if there is a spirit of *confusion*, then it does not have the Spirit of God! The Word says, "Satan is the author of confusion," not God. Within days the principal from my children's Christian school asked me to pray about teaching at the school! There would be a substantial cut in pay but I would have my evenings, weekends and summers with my kids.

Immediately, I applied for the position, did the interview, was offered and accepted the teaching job at my children's school. My family was ecstatic. God even worked out a smooth transition from my other jobs. In the weeks following my acceptance, God allowed me to see His confirmations all around me. Then, after a wonderful summer with my family as a 'full-time' mom again, God asked me to do one other thing. He had sent a new senior pastor to our church, and God was asking me to step down from *all* ministries at the church and *wait* for Him. I could not believe God could tell a person to do this. So, I hesitated. Suddenly, all the ministries I was involved in started falling apart! Confusion was back. This time I recognized it! Again, He asked me to give up all the ministries at church and *rest* in His shadow.

Once school started I realized why He had instructed me to step out of all other ministries and rest. It was more than a teaching job— teaching in a Christian school is the toughest ministry I had ever tackled.

Back at the conference in Chicago with my friend, I remember clearly hearing the Holy Spirit speaking to my heart saying, "It's time to come out of my shadow now…your work must begin." I felt God asking me to once again start speaking to ladies' groups, help my husband in lay ministry wherever he is lead, and to work with a group of young teenaged girls at the high school with a fitness group. I remember telling Him, "thanks for giving me ministries which are my strengths! I can do it, Lord!"

Later that night my friend, Jill, and I were swimming in the pool. I told her all about my new commitment to God's calling. Since Jill and I were summer "work-out buddies," we decided to do laps in the water to make up for the decadent chocolate cake we indulged in at supper. Both having a playfully competitive nature, we took off. Boom! A muscle spasm hit my legs taking me by complete surprise.

"Leg cramp," I thought. "I must not be in as good of shape as I thought." We both laughed. And I shook it out. Except it wouldn't shake out. Both legs went into muscle spasms. My leg muscles were spasming all night long. Suddenly, in the course of one night, everything in my life became an effort—including putting on makeup, peeling potatoes, writing on the whiteboard at school, even lifting my hands to praise—because the muscles in my forearms also became affected.

The muscles would hurt so badly at night that to sleep I started taking cold medicine to knock me out. The next day my arms and legs would be the same. By the beginning of November, I started having cognitive problems in which I could not remember new material, my speech was slurring while I was teaching a lesson, and I was having problems thinking of words. I felt stupid!

There was one fear in the back of my mind. Eight years before I had experienced similar problems. I went to my doctor who sent me to a neurologist; however, before testing could really be done, the symptoms subsided totally. I claimed healing from whatever neurological problem I was having. When I went back to the neurologist, he believed there was a good chance I had Multiple Sclerosis. I rebuked the very thought of it! I was not going down that road! God had healed me! He flippantly said as I left his office, "…you are in remission…I will see you again…you will be back!" I hated him for that.

Perhaps that is why I did not want to go to the doctor this time. It could not be *that. God had healed me!* God's healing is for keeps. His healing is not temporary. I tried to ignore the problems. The spasms—the cognitive problems—the speech problems—even now a vision problem—fatigue was sickening.

Finally, December 8 (just two days before my 21st wedding anniversary) the symptoms almost completely stopped. The neurologist took another MRI. Finally, admitting there were no visible brain lesions, but standing behind a preliminary diagnosis of *probable* MS. Probable MS? To me that is not a diagnosis. It is hope—hope that it is *not* MS! "Besides God healed once…He can heal again," I remember claiming.

I had to get back to my focus of the fresh vision God had called me to. The girls' fitness group was going well…until I got sick. Now I was going to work on getting my muscles built up again. However, each time I went with them to work out after school, I would not be able to keep up—I was even having problems keeping balance on the recovery stations.

My speech had not improved. I did not tell my students about my illness, so my speech became a joke between us. For some reason I thought it better to be considered "absent-minded" rather than to be pitied because of illness. Besides, contracts would be coming due. I really wanted to continue my ministry at the school.

My husband was there with me in the middle of the night rubbing my legs and arms when my muscles would cramp up. He was the one that would hold me in his arms and let me cry. Although at first I wanted to shelter him from this disease, I realized it wasn't just me that had it—WE had it! Eric and I and our entire family and friends! We would have to rely on and pray for each other to get through this tough time.

During praise and worship at church I reached my hands up to God and just tried praising Him; however, after just a few moments I realized, I could not keep my hands up...so I lowered my hands and tried to keep singing. I made up my mind that no matter what, I would praise the Lord; however, I was really struggling. At that point I felt an arm around me. My friend, Jill, was suddenly there hugging me. She whispered in my ear, "No matter what this is, I will be here for you. We will get through this." Then she cried with me.

God had sent her there at the time I needed a girlfriend most. We stood there praising God together—praising with a song of hope. God had shown me that I had my husband by my side, but God knew I needed someone more. Even Moses had two who helped him hold up his rod when he grew weary. God knew I was struggling at that moment...He is always on time just when we need Him most.

Later that night, after the service, I prayed at the altar. I realized that Satan was attacking me in every area I had told God I would serve Him in. How could I serve Him with the fitness club if my muscles would not allow me to exercise? How could I talk to women's groups if I stammer and have slurred speech? How could I minister with my husband if I can't get around? "God," I prayed, "You called me in areas I love to serve. You called me in areas of my strengths. I committed all of my strengths to you...I don't understand what is going on." It was at that point I felt Him say, "You gave me your strengths...but will you give me your weaknesses?" I realize that I had done just that. It is easy to commit to God what you are good at...that comes easy. But the sacrifice comes in struggles and trials of weakness. "Yes, God." I prayed. "Take every part of me...my strengths and my weaknesses...for you are my strength when I am weak."

Visits to the neurologists became a semi-monthly event. On one particular visit, my friend went with me instead of my husband because it

19

was a "routine" visit. However, it was then that the doctor gave me the diagnosis that the disease I was struggling with was early-onset Parkinson's disease. I felt like saying, "Can I go back to MS?" My friend spoke up and asked questions. I just kept silent. I had barely known of two people with it—enough to know that the disease does not shorten your lifespan, it just robs you of every movement, every blink, every word— leaving just a shell to live on. Eventually, it would even rob its victim of his smile. What a maddening disease. How unfair!

My doctor sent me to the Mayo Clinic to get a second opinion. Disappointedly, the diagnosis was the same. I had to trust in God. He knew before the beginning of time that Tammie Judd would have early-onset Parkinson's at the age of 42. I may not understand "why," but I can understand that I trust Him, He is good, and He loves me. This is living in faith...this is where the rubber meets the road.

The doctor had asked me if I had a good support system. I have an excellent support system—a wonderful, loving husband who would always be by my side no matter what may come. He reaffirmed that over and over again. I have five amazing children. Although at first we thought we could 'shelter' them from this, we realized they needed to know the truth. Having two grown children made it easier because they understood more of what was going on in my life and helped the younger ones to understand. Fortunately, I was responding to the medication well, I was symptom-free virtually all the time.

One thing about a chronic illness is that it is at best unpredictable. One day you may not get out of bed, the next day you feel 'great' (relatively speaking). Then you try to plan tomorrow or next week or next month and WHAM! You have a setback. This is what was so frustrating about the disease—its inconsistency. It is so true what the scriptures say in Proverbs 16:9 "A man's heart plans his way, but the LORD directs his steps."

As I started getting ready for school, I got more and more angry. It took twice as long to do anything. By the time the kids got downstairs, I was taking it out on them. When I tried to apologize to my family...it just ended in anger. It wasn't until I got to school and really prayed again I realized that I was struggling with anger. That is alright to admit to God. So many times we only come to God with praise or to tell Him good things or to ask for something. But, if God is truly our friend and our Father, we need to come to Him with every emotion. He knows our heart anyway.

Why do we have the Adam-and-Eve complex and try to hide? During my prayer I told God that I was MAD! Then I realized I was mad at Him! He allowed me to see that I was angry because I was disappointed!

I was disappointed because I needed to know that the rules of health apply here—if you eat right (which I did) and exercise (which I did) and take your vitamins (which I did) you will wake up every morning feeling youthful and vivacious. I was angry because I had plans for my life, and it did not include unpredictable health.

I was disappointed that His healing eight years ago was gone! I was angry because everything always came easy for me in school and in life—now *everything* was difficult! I was MAD because I felt I was not in control of the situation! But it was when I admitted that I was really in control of nothing, that I realized God is in control of everything—and that is all I needed.

> *What Satan didn't realize was that in every trial he gave me, he actually was giving me wonderful material to speak to women...and to spread the Gospel.*

I am so happy I am *not* in control—I would really louse things up. I cried out to God how much I loved Him. Once again I gave Him total control. His love flooded into my soul as I cried...still tears of disappointment and a little anger...but knowing His promises (Rom. 8:28). Jeremiah 29:11 came to me, '"For I alone know the plans I have for you," said the Lord. "They are plans for good and not for evil, to give a future and a *hope*."'

God sees the whole picture—we don't. He is the creator of this painting we call life...and we are His masterpiece. What Satan didn't realize was that in every trial he gave me, he actually was giving me wonderful material to speak to women...and to spread the Gospel. What Satan was hitting me with would be used to minister. Even my family would be bound together tighter now! My husband and I are closer than ever! My friends have really proven what a gift they are! What a fool Satan is! I realize now that this is NOT a stop sign on the road of life—it is only a bump!

❧4❧

DOREEN HANNA

True Hidden Treasure?

I t was a cool spring evening; I finished the dishes and headed outside to speak with my husband in hopes of engaging in a friendly conversation. Arriving in his presence he began to rage over the neighbor's use of a noisy power saw. It seemed that he was angry over everything those days, big or small. In the last few months, with each outburst of anger, I felt like another valve of my heart slammed shut and the coldness of my own unspoken anger and resentment set in deeper.

That evening as I walked alone down by the oceanfront, my thoughts turned to a class I taught for several years on "Understanding Him and I." In the last several months I tried every suggestion I had given to others. Where were the answers to my own problems? We'd been married for 24 years; shouldn't I have all the answers by now?

Upon my return home from my beachfront walk, we received a phone call from a long time friend. The purpose of his call that night was to inform us that he was interested in coming to visit us. While he and my husband were conversing, my heart leaped with excitement. My mind rushed back to our good-bye ten years ago. "If anything ever happens to Chad or if he treats you or the girls badly, I'll be there for you."

It was like I had rushed to that hidden box I had placed in the recesses of my heart many years ago. Now for the first time, I was opening the lid to my secret treasure. I reminisced on his last good-bye kiss and whispering those words of reassurance. Now, where darkness had been hovering in my heart, I felt something foreign – Hope! It felt like light had dispelled the darkness. Hope that his coming would bring some joy, passion, or fulfillment into my life. We made plans that evening for him to come at the time of our youngest daughter's high school graduation.

For several days after his call, I savored the short conversation we had. He had reminded me that he still hadn't found the woman "like me" he had been looking for. Pride engulfed me. I had been feeling so unappreciated at home that any small recognition seemed larger than life. I was desperate for acknowledgment; hungry for anyone to say I was a woman of value.

In the ensuing months prior to his arrival I was consumed by my fantasy. It was more powerful than a romance novel. It began to emotionally distance and further harden my heart towards my husband. I began to spend less and less time with God.

His arrival came quickly. As he stepped off the plane his greeting was all that I had hoped for, a warm hug and kiss.

Our houseguest's three-day visit gave me everything I had wanted to hear and feel. He'd tell me how pretty I still was, how well I managed a home, how bright I was, and give many stolen kisses. I loved hearing every tantalizing word. I felt warm, wanted, and valued. I pictured us in Hawaii, Cabo, Texas…anywhere that was far away from my miserable marriage.

In the evening of the last day of his visit, we were finally alone after everyone else had gone to bed. I was so obsessed in our passionate embrace that I neglected to consider that Chad might not be asleep. Suddenly I heard Chad's voice, "That's enough! Either take him to a hotel or take him to the airport, just get him out of here."

As we walked into the hotel lobby a cold and deep void overwhelmed me. *How had I allowed myself to come this far?* I had left our youngest daughter at home with her father – a very angry man! *What would my oldest daughter, Brandy, think of her mother now?*

I pushed aside my guilty and fearful thoughts as I walked into the room, focusing on how I had been mentally and emotionally fulfilled in the last few days. Now I finally attained the moment wherein the pinnacle of my fantasies were going to be fulfilled.

I was lost in my own thoughts when I heard him call my name. "Doreen, please listen to me. I will always be grateful to Chad, because he spared my life tonight. He has been like a big brother to me and I have betrayed him. I have caused you to violate your marriage vows enough already. I have been trying to get my life right with God and right now I am not going to follow through and have sex with you… I have to STAND FIRM."

Those two words rang so loud in my ears it was deafening and a cold chill ran down my spine. My mind began to reel, remembering how many times in the last months I had heard those same words…

As I crested the top of the church stairs where our Pastor stood to greet everyone coming in, he asked me where Chad had been. I shared with him that Chad had chosen not to attend church any longer. He quickly reassured me that he'd be praying for us.

As I took my place in the sanctuary I soon felt an arm around my shoulder; it was Pastor Zac, giving me a hug of comfort. As he was about to walk away he quickly pivoted back around and then looked me straight in the eye, with those *piercing blue eyes* and stated, "Remember to STAND FIRM." I was taken aback by his words and weakly replied, "I am." I pondered his words then and thought, "How could he say such a thing?" I *am* the one "standing firm" in this marriage right now!

In the next few days I thought about Pastor Zac's challenge. I was puzzled, because I felt that I was standing firm. *I wasn't planning on leaving Chad, I was the one who had called for counseling; I wasn't the one raging in anger, I was the one who was trying to just keep things together and not let anybody know what was really going on.*

On the following Thursday of that same week I received a call from a dear friend asking me to meet her for dinner. Over dessert she began to tell me that she had a dream about me the prior evening. In her dream she saw me dressed in the armor of God, and she heard the Lord speaking to me "STAND FIRM." I shivered as she stated the words. I asked her if she had seen or spoken to Zac and she said that she had been out of town the prior weekend, and had not been in contact with him upon her return. We were both in awe of God's specific word for me and she encouraged me strongly to keep watch for what might cause me to stumble. I walked from the restaurant to the car that evening amazed at how specifically and loudly God was speaking to me.

I was continuing to reflect on how in the last few months I seemed to have had many "STAND FIRM" encounters, when I heard him call my name; which whirled me back to my present circumstance.

I was stunned by the realization of what a miraculous encounter I was having. God was speaking to me in this hotel room, wherein I was with another man, and in the midst of what I felt at that moment was my greatest sin! I didn't know whether I should laugh, cry, or just Stand Up! It was all too unbelievable.

I was disappointed that my passion wouldn't be satisfied. I was not only embarrassed by his apparent righteousness but also feared what my act of open rebellion in front of Chad was going to bring. By this time, passion had diminished for both of us. We talked till the early morning hours about what my choices might be from this point on.

I then took him to the airport. He stated that this would be the last time we would ever see or speak to each other again. He said that we must abide by what the Bible says "If your right eye causes you to sin, gouge it out and if your right hand causes you to sin, cut if off..." He boarded the plane and never looked back. From the airport I called my sister who lived close by and asked if I could come and stay with her a few days. She graciously consented. I then called and asked my father if it would be possible for me to come and stay with him and mom in Phoenix, AZ for a period of time, until I could sort things out.

Within days I was kissing my girls goodbye and flying to Arizona, finding the foothills a place of refuge. I spent many evenings walking the dirt roads by my parent's home, hearing the coyotes howl at night and the quail call in the morning. The comfort of loving parents and having my meals prepared for me was such a refreshing change from all the demands of my own household.

Yet, my heart ached in hopelessness, it pounded heavily every time I thought about my girls; it grew cold as I thought of Chad. I remember walking down one of those dirt paths one evening and the song "Change my heart oh God, make it ever true," literally came out of my mouth. I stopped immediately and told the Lord that I couldn't sing that song, because I didn't want to be true to Him or Chad at that time; and if going back to Chad was His will, I wasn't willing.

I quickly pursued getting a job and quickly saved up the money to file for a divorce. Several months later, one Sunday morning, now attending church upon the insistence of a true friend, another woman who had also befriended me, asked if I would like to attend a women's Bible study she would be facilitating.

The first night of the Bible study I found myself in the midst of nine other ladies who were widowed, divorced, or separated. I thought, *I should feel right at home here.* But I was miserable throughout the evening and couldn't figure out why.

I went to bed crying that night and willing for the first time to ask the Lord "Why? Why do I feel so confused and miserable?" I heard God speak to my heart, "I've been waiting for you to be willing." Shivers slid down my spine, as I knew God had not spoken to me this clearly in a very long time.

My thoughts immediately returned to that evening when I first arrived in Arizona, and how I so boldly told the Lord, "If Your will is for me to return to Chad, I'm not willing." Now, hearing the voice of God, I knew I must choose to obey or harden my heart further. With my respect of God, and knowing the consequences of continual sin, I began to think, "Would Chad be willing to accept me back now?"

While I was contemplating how I would approach Chad, the thought came to my mind that I would use the opportunity of our oldest daughter's wedding, which was just weeks away, as an excuse to speak with him while I was in California. I called Chad that evening and asked if we could meet while I was in town. He invited me to *his new home* for dinner.

My time spent in the word seemed to provide words of grace and forgiveness; reminding me continually of His love and faithfulness.

In the days prior to my arrival, I asked God to give me a sign that Chad might be willing to consider reconciliation. I arrived in California feeling very anxious. The morning of the day I was to have dinner with him I picked up my youngest daughter so that we could have some time alone together. She jumped in the car and the first thing she said was, "Dad's making you a really nice dinner Mom—filet mignon and strawberry shortcake." I looked up toward heaven and said, "Hmmm, not bad, Lord." When I arrived that evening, Chad opened the door with a smile on his face and warmth in his eyes. That was my sign; I hadn't seen that warmth in his eyes in years.

I knew I couldn't wait until after strawberry shortcake to say what I had to say. So, after a short exchange on the weather, I blurted out "Chad, how would you feel if I told you I would be willing to consider reconciliation?" He began to cry uncontrollably. In those moments of his gaining composure, I thought of every worse scenario. And then I heard him say, "This is the answer to prayer I've been waiting for." I ran to him and we embraced, now weeping together. With his arms wrapped around me, I felt warm in my heart, relieved in my mind and tingly all the way to my toes. We sat down and enjoyed the wonderful dinner that he had prepared. We talked and cried, then laughed and cried. Before I left that evening, Chad took me by the hand and we prayed together for the first time in many years.

For the next four months we worked towards reconciliation. Chad asked the obvious question, "What really happened that night after you left the house?" I felt cold, afraid, even strange, talking about that night to the very one I had betrayed. I expressed how I had felt "already divorced" from him emotionally, therefore justifying my actions to be fulfilled physically; even though we had not culminated our passion completely.

Chad, in turn, shared openly about how he had attended a Promise Keepers event, which had put life in perspective for him while we were apart. Chad was able to admit that achieving his ultimate career goal a few years before our separation left him feeling lonely at the top. His desire for success did not bring the happiness he had hoped for. Therefore, turning to those who didn't care about his Christian walk, he pursued drinking as a substitute for comfort. Hearing him share things with such transparency was healing to my mind and emotions. I returned to Chad six weeks prior to our final divorce court date.

In those early months of our joyful reunion I remember attending "concerts in the park" and we would dance in the street as the music played. It was so romantic. I also rejoiced and felt the warmth of us growing close to each other as we prayed with transparency together daily.

> *I must admit there were times when I was fearful because it appeared that "some things had never changed."*

I must admit there were times when I was fearful because it appeared that "some things had never changed." Like, Chad being late from work. This would create such fear in my heart; this was a real lack of trust issue for me. I would be thinking, "Where is he? What is he doing? Whom might he be with?"

However, when I would address my fear in prayer and remember that God is greater than any fear I had II Timothy 1:7 would come to mind, "I have not given you a spirit of fear, but of power, love and sound mind." My fears would be arrested not only by the reassurance of God's presence but also by the beautiful bouquet of flowers that Chad had often stopped to buy for me.

Today, the temptations for Chad and I to find comforts elsewhere have decreased as time and continual acts of faithfulness have re-established the bond of trust between us. Today, Chad and I enjoy the pleasure of reconciled relationships between family and friends; something we value as a precious treasure.

Our freedom from shame has often times given us opportunities to share our story with others who are considering separation or divorce. Our desire is that something in our story will give people hope and encourage them to seek God and His will for their lives.

May I encourage you to "Stand Firm" in the midst of whatever trial you may be going through and remember always, God's faithfulness—it is the greatest treasure you and I can possess.

⇜5⇝

FEONA SHARHRAN HUFF

Courage Under Fire: A Single Mom's Journey to Empowerment

"I had some good days/I had some hills to climb/I had some weary days/And some lonely nights/But then I look around/And I think things over/All of my good days/Outweigh my bad days/I won't complain"
--stanza from gospel song, *I Won't Complain*

What do you do when you've lost your job, you're pending eviction, the kitchen cabinets are nearly bare, you've got a shut-off utility notice, your growing kids need new shoes, and the bank account is tapped out? Here's what I did: I put aside my pride for the well-being and stability of my daughter and son and applied for public assistance (Otherwise known to most as "welfare"). That's right... Feona Sharhran Huff—a college graduate with a journalism career that includes published articles in *Essence, Black Enterprise, Upscale,* and *The Virginian-Pilot*—had to rely on "the system" for help.

I remember the day I made my way to the welfare office. The majority of the women who I saw, with strollers and toddlers in tow, were standing in line for the same reason I was. Many of them looked perplexed and worried. They seemed stressed and frustrated. How could you blame them? Any time you try to get assistance from the government you're bound to run into red tape and lots of headaches.

I cried out to the Lord, "Why me, Lord? Why did I have to be in this financial situation and have to come down to a place like this where people behind the counter as well as the caseworkers try their best to strip you of your dignity, pride, and self esteem just because you need help?" I mean, it's not like I didn't have anything going for myself. I lost my job and was getting freelancing work while seeking other employment. However, the checks were coming in sporadically and I needed financial stability to maintain rent and my other bills.

There would have been a time that I would have been ashamed to admit this truth, especially because people have always held me in high regard and I wouldn't want to disappoint them. Plus, I have family members who would be more than happy to know that my life wasn't perfect and that I had experienced tough times, and wouldn't want to give them the satisfaction of getting wind of this information. However, I am crystal clear that my temporary situation is not who I am. Therefore, I am disclosing this very personal part of my life to let other single moms know that, despite what they are going through, it's only temporary and as long as God gives us the gift of life and breath, we have the opportunity to change our circumstances with courage, faith, and an action plan. I no longer care who knows the challenges I've faced because if what I've gone through can empower just one single mom, then my sharing was not in vain.

I remember many times when I had to show courage under fire such as the times when I didn't have any money and I had to get my son to school. It wouldn't have been a problem if my three year old attended school within our community because I could have walked him there in minutes flat. Instead, his school was an hour away by foot. But rather than have my son miss out on learning and socialization time with his classmates, which was very important at his age, I strapped him in the stroller and walked him to school. I adjusted my attitude and calmed my spirit to see the brighter side of things: I had feet to walk the distance, the weather was decent, and it allowed me to take in some exercise as well as bonding time. Plus, I discovered new stores that I could make a connection with regarding my magazines.

And then, there were times when money was tight and I chose to walk to my destinations just so that I would have the money to buy the kids snacks after school. Being able to do this meant a lot to me. I never wanted my children to go without even the simplest thing if I could make arrangements to have the resources in place.

I truly believe that it takes a strong woman to handle the role of a single mom because it's no joke. It's been the most challenging yet rewarding role I've held to date. You have to be everything to your children: Mother, father, nurturer, teacher, disciplinarian, cheerleader, counselor, etc. If the father is providing some support, that's excellent. But for most of us that's not the case. Therefore, we have to be empowered and up for the challenges that lie ahead of us because they are sure to come. What has kept me centered throughout the good days and hard times is my faith in God. His Word promises that He will never leave or forsake me. I constantly ask the Lord to help me and give me the strength to raise my children as He desires me to do so. I call on Him for instruction, patience, and tolerance.

> *If the father is providing some support, that's excellent. But for most of us that's not the case.*

I usually don't get emotional in front of my children because I know they feed off of my emotions, but one day I just couldn't help it. I was coming down on myself because I didn't feel like I was being enough or had enough materialistic things to give them. My spirit was hurting and I couldn't contain the tears. Suddenly, my son put his arms around my waist and said, "Don't worry, Mommy. It will be okay." My daughter then came up to me and said that she loved me, as tears began to fill her eyes. What that moment revealed to me was that my children truly loved me. It didn't matter that I didn't have the money to buy them what I thought was important at the time. Their hugs and encouraging words reminded me that the greatest gift I could give them was loving them and being there for them. And now, they were being there for me.

While I have faced some challenging days in my journey as a single mom, I've had some great days. As a child, I always knew that I was going to produce a magazine, but what kind I didn't know. About three months after my daughter was born, so was my magazine. A friend of mine, DeAnthony, had stopped by to check on us. At the time, I was working on an article for Upscale Magazine. He said, "You're always working on articles for everyone else. Why don't you start your own?" I told him that I didn't have the money but he assured me that that should not be a deterrent. He had just seen a woman selling her poetry magazine on the train. After mulling the idea over, the idea of a magazine for single moms came to mind. The next day, I called my journalism colleagues and put the word out that I was producing Solo Mommy Magazine.

Since 2001, the publication, which went from solely being online to now being in print, has been empowering single moms with strategies to help them live simpler, less stressed lives. In 2005, I held my 1st Annual

Mother's Day Brunch in which I awarded five single moms with the "You Go, Mom" award. I started this event because I wanted to celebrate single moms who were the epitome of strength, courage, tenacity, and savviness. Single moms from throughout the United States as well as in other countries, including Australia, have reached out to me and praised me for the work I am doing.

Just as the magazine is helping them, it's helping me as well. When I get emails or letters from single moms who have been going through ordeals and when they discover Solo Mommy they feel encouraged. That lets me know that my efforts are not in vain. I know that God has given me an incredible writing talent and the ability to find resources that would be beneficial to the women I'm serving, and so, I do the very best I can. I believe in supporting my fellow single moms and that's what the magazine does.

I involve my children in everything that I do and I expose them to all of my gifts. Right now, my daughter is proficient on the computer and is an awesome artist. Her artwork graces the cover of my first children's book *But We're a Family, Too*. She is the editor of the *Just For Us* department in Solo Mommy Magazine. My son was the catalyst and inspiration behind my second magazine, Black Boy. I've named him as the Co-Publisher and President. One day, he's going to take over the magazine. Right now, he's growing into his inheritance and will learn every facet of the business as he develops and grows. Not only does this forge a bond between me and my children, but it's equally teaching them about business and entrepreneurship. That way, they can decide when they get older if they want to work for someone else or for themselves. The key? They've got options!

I have had a lot of support in my seven years of being a single mom. Tanya Samuels, Matthew Scott, Maurice Spigner, Kathy White, and Lenny Matthews are just a few people who have stood by me through thick and thin. Tanya has watched my kids so I could go to work. Matthew has been there for me for trips to the ER to bring me Metro Cards, give me some extra funds to do stuff for the kids, and just to be there for a shoulder to cry on. Maurice has picked me up to take the kids to school, put food in the house, and done whatever was necessary to ensure that we were comfortable. Kathy has sent money for the kids and been an encouraging sister. Lenny, who was one of my first mentors when I moved to New York ten years ago, has always been my support whenever I called on him no matter what time of the day or night it was. I count these individuals as my family. I love them and I truly thank God for placing them in my life.

In closing, I just want all you single moms reading my story to know that you are not alone in the struggle. Times may get hard but I'm here to tell you that the storm won't last but for a season. There may be times when you doubt your ability to make things happen for you and your kids, but you've got to shake off that negative thinking and remember that you are more than a conqueror. God has empowered you to carry out your role. It's only when you display courage under fire that you can have a testimony to share with the next single mom who crosses your path to help her get through her challenges as hopefully my testimony is able to do for you.

ᴂ6ᴈ

SHELLY BROWN

Bring Back My Mom!

Yet I will rejoice in the Lord, I will joy in the God of my salvation. The Lord God is my strength; He will make my feet like deer's feet, And He will make me walk on my high hills (Habakkuk 3:18-19).

I couldn't believe my eyes! It was the most beautiful home I'd ever seen. I walked with my new parents and brother through the beautifully stained front door. Holding on to the handcrafted banister, I excitedly bounced up each step. After about twelve wonderful steps we arrived on the main living area of our new home. My *new* dad took my hand and asked, "Honey, do you want to see your bedroom?"

In eager anticipation I tugged at his hands as we turned and walked up another flight of stairs. My bedroom was on the third floor of this amazing house. I stood in the doorway of my new room and in amazement took in every inch. It was green! Bright green! I walked in and sat on the chair at my very own desk touching every inch with the palm of my hands. There was just one bed in the room and it was mine, mine alone. I couldn't believe I had my very own room. I was a princess in my very own fairytale. Or so I thought …

Just a year before, I was chasing an ambulance down our driveway. It was taking away my mom. She wasn't supposed to die. Sure, she suffered many injuries from the car accident, but she could live with her paralysis. Then out of nowhere the unexpected happened. She developed a blood infection and died three days later.

As the ambulance pulled away with her, I ran after it as fast as I possibly could, screaming and crying, "BRING BACK MY MOMMY!

PLEASE BRING MY MOMMY BACK!" Much to my surprise the ambulance stopped. The driver got out and walked back to where I was standing. I thought he was going to bring back my mom but he stopped simply to tell me to stop running. He said, "Honey, you're going to hurt yourself running like that." He motioned for my grandmother to come and help me. Together we stood there as they continued their journey down our driveway. I needed my mom and they were taking her away from me. Crushed and dying inside, I helplessly watched as they faded from my view.

The funeral was five days later. I walked into the chapel and saw her laying in her casket. Immediately, I rushed up to her and softly laid my hand on her hands gently shaking her as if it would wake her. Then I began to cry, "Mommy, please wake up. You have to wake up mommy! I need you. Please, please wake up." She didn't wake up. My aunt walked up to me and removed my hand from my mom's hand, gently leading me to a front row seat where I sat next to my dad. The funeral ended almost as quickly as it began.

As the visitors filed out of the room my dad took a moment and knelt down by me kissing me on the cheek. He said, "goodbye" and I never saw him again.

After the funeral my adult cousins took my brother, sisters and me to live with them for a few months. With five members in their own family and then four additional children living in a single-wide three bedroom trailer the frustration level was understandably at an all time high.

The first night I lay in my bed crying for my mom. I missed her so terribly, and I needed her to hug and kiss me goodnight. I suppose I was crying too loudly because my cousin came tearing into the bedroom and scolded me, "STOP! Stop crying now! If you cry for your mom again, I'll give you something to cry about!" It only took a couple of times of discipline to assure me that she meant business. I made sure I didn't cry when they were around, but each night, deep into my pillow I cried for my mom. I needed her and I needed her touch. I needed her protection and I needed her love. It hurt so badly to know that I'd never experience it again.

Three months later my brother and I were placed in state custody. We were welcomed with open arms by our new foster family. They seemed really nice ... but that too would soon end. By the end of the first week my foster father began to abuse me almost daily. This abuse lasted for nine long months.

Finally, nearly a year after my mom died, word came that a childless couple wanted to adopt me and my brother. We were so excited at the thought of a "forever mom and dad."

Indeed ... I was a princess in my very own fairytale ... for two short weeks.

My new dad was amazing. He was nearly 40 years old and finally had the opportunity to be a dad to his very own son and daughter. He lived each day to come home to talk with us and play with us and read to us.

Life with our new mom was quite a different story. After about two weeks she became very jealous of the relationship that had formed between us and our dad. Perhaps she felt left out, perhaps she felt that she could not compete for the love and need that we still had for our birth mom. Unfortunately, she gave up too early.

I remember the day as if it were yesterday. Even at the very young age of seven, I remember the feeling of complete devastation, almost as though I'd lost my mom all over again. The words still echo in my mind ...

"I am your 'real' mom," she said. "Your birth mom is gone. From this day on you *will* call me 'mom.' You *will* refer to me as your 'real' mom."

I wasn't ready to call her mom. At my young age I was unable to articulate why, but I knew that I still missed my birth mom, and I still needed her. I called my new dad, "dad" about a week after I was adopted. It was very natural for me. My natural father wasn't around much before my mom died. It wasn't a difficult transition to a dad that immediately showed his love and attention to me. I wasn't ready to call my new mom, "mom." I'm sure it would have happened eventually and naturally, but it was forced on me. And how dare she tell me she was now my 'real' mom. I remember walking away from her desperately angry and hurting, longing for my *real* mom.

> *The life I so desperately longed for collapsed before it could even begin.*

Instead of earning my love and respect she demanded it. Feeling out of control she spent the next four years physically, emotionally and mentally abusing me and my brother. The life I so desperately longed for collapsed before it could even begin. The very mom that chose me apparently decided that I did not measure up to her expectations, so she chose to reject me on every level.

Finally, my parents divorced. Fearing for our lives my dad fought for custody of me and my brother, and won.

Thirty-one years later, at 38, I am happily married with three amazing children. Through godly mentors and through the Word of God, miraculous healing has taken place in my life. Healing began when I studied God's love letter to me (Psalm 139), and Romans 8:28.

After reading Psalm 139 over and over and over again I was finally convinced that God loves me ... yes me! I always knew that God loved the "world." John 3:16 so clearly states that. But to me, the world was everyone else but me. There was no possible way that God could love me ... the abused, rejected and abandoned me. No possible way! However, once I finally allowed the knowledge of the love of God to penetrate my heart I began to experience the miraculous healing I longed to experience for so long.

Once I began to trust that God really loves me, I needed to come to terms with the circumstances of my past. I began to study Romans chapter 8. I came across a very familiar verse, Romans 8:28.

It says in part, "All things work together for good to those who love the Lord..." I came to understand that ALL THINGS, means *ALL THINGS*- all circumstances good or bad. All people problems, all sin, ALL THINGS work together.

A deeper study of that verse revealed two more very important facts. First, this is a promise to "those who love the Lord," a promise to believers, a promise to me! Second, this is a promise that God will take ALL things and literally overrule them by turning them into something GOOD! That means that God will take your past sin and literally overrule it and turn it into something good. It means that God will take all my past circumstances and turn them into something good. That is a promise to those who love the Lord!

Are you struggling with your past? Worried about your future? Hurting over present pain in your life? Are you living in a famine, be it financial, spiritual or emotional?

When your thoughts are filled with doubt or fear and your world seems to be collapsing around you remember the words of Habakkuk. Regardless of his circumstances he learned that fear could be turned into faith when he depended on his Heavenly Father:

"Though the fig tree may not blossom, Nor fruit be on the vines; Though the labor of the olive may fail, And the fields yield no food; Though the flock may be cut off from the fold, And there be no herd in the stalls – Yet I will rejoice in the Lord, I will joy in the God of my salvation The Lord God is my strength; He will make my feet like deer's feet, And He will make me walk on my high hills" (Habakkuk 3:17-19).

❧7❧

Trish Jones
Isaiah 43:
18-19

TRISH JONES

Standing Unashamed

It was a Sunday morning in September 2003, and Pastor Pete, the Senior Pastor of our Church was speaking on "Getting the Stink Out of Your Life," a recount of the story of Lazarus, whom Jesus raised from the dead.

He talked about how Jesus didn't mind the stench coming from Lazarus's grave. He used this as an analogy of us opening up about the secret things of our past that could be eating away at us and causing a "stench" in our lives.

I couldn't wait until the meeting was over, and it wasn't because I was thinking about the "stink" in my life. No, I was actually excited because I knew my mum, whom I love deeply, had lived with a secret ever since I was conceived—and in my view, it was time for her to be released from carrying that burden.

On a Mission

When I left Church that day, I was on a mission to set my mother free.

A few days later, I was driving through the village near my home and I was so upbeat. The sun was shining and I was thinking about what it was going to be like for my mum when she could finally let go of her past.

I was so happy for her that I was smiling from my heart as I sang. But then all of a sudden my optimistic mood was interrupted with an audible voice that said, "It's not your mum I'm concerned about, it's you." I didn't need to ask who was speaking or what this statement meant, but the voice was so audible that I turned my head toward the rear passenger

37

seats of the car and said "No Lord, never ever...Never going to tell anyone that story. I've always been happy just sharing that part of my life with You and now You want me to go and tell other people?" In such a gentle way, God responded, "But you're not happy though are you?"

There was no doubt in my mind that what God was saying was right, because this secret had haunted my marriage for fourteen years. But, this didn't stop the awful pain and guilt that I was now feeling. And, neither did it stop me bargaining with God—and bargain I did!

I told God that since I was planning a trip to the U.S. to visit my coach, I'd wait until then and tell her. But every time I spoke to her, the date was pushed back. I had to learn that when God wants you to do something, He will use every available means to ensure you obey Him, and obey Him on His terms.

My fear of rejection from other people didn't help, but it seemed as though every time I turned the TV on or spoke to someone, the issue of "facing your fears or telling the truth" seemed to slap me in my face.

Today is the Day

One Sunday morning, weeks after God challenged me to speak out, I was upstairs in my office speaking to my Great Aunt over the telephone, and she said "husbands and wives shouldn't have any secrets." She wasn't even talking about my marriage, but it hit me like a lead bolt and I was compelled to cut my conversation with her short. By the time I hung up the telephone, my legs were like jelly, my heart started racing and I'm saying to God, "I really don't know how I'm going to be able to do this, but I know today is the day."

My Bible was lying on my desk so I asked God to show me what to do. I opened it up, and what I read said something to the effect of "I'm not going to tell you what you should do, because you know you should do it." My response was "thank you Lord for your support ... not!"

I started walking towards the door of my office and then I stopped because I was so nervous and I kept asking myself if I was doing the right thing. But then the strangest thing happened...I heard myself shout "Chris! Chris!" It was a cry of despair, and by this time it was too late to retract what I was about to tell him.

Chris, my husband, came running out of the kitchen as I got half way down stairs and by this time, I'm crying inconsolably—almost as if I were delirious. And he said "Trish, what's wrong?" I said "I've got something to tell you, and you're not going to like this, to which he responded, "Nothing could ever be that bad."

38

By this time, I'd reached the bottom of the stairs, and he held me by the shoulders and ushered me into the dining room and rearranged the chairs so that we were sitting facing each other. He then said "Come on, tell me, what's the problem?"

As I sat there shaking, I had to tell my husband of 14 years, that in my mid-teens I'd suffered relentless abuse. Before I had a chance to expand on what I was telling him, he put his arms around me and said "I love you more than I've ever loved you before."

I let out the deepest sob, because it was the answer I so desperately wanted, but it was also the answer I so deeply felt I didn't deserve. In fact, a part of me felt worse because he hadn't punished me for not telling him before we were married. Instead of being angry with me, here he was squeezing me tight and telling me how much he loved me.

I had everything to lose that day, but in doing what God had commanded me to do, I lost nothing, but I gained everything. I learned that it was safe to follow God's orders and I'm so grateful for His faithfulness.

Compassion for Others

Because of the sensitive way in which Chris dealt with this situation, I felt strong enough to now tell some close members of my family, all of whom were very supportive. But over the coming months, there were times when I still felt so low because I was now feeling guilty about not having told Chris sooner.

One day as I was praying, I said "God, you have to explain to me, why it took me so many years to tell Chris? I feel like an impostor, and he deserves better!"

It wasn't until about three weeks later that my answer came. As I opened the refrigerator, the Holy Spirit said, "Because I want you to understand what other people have been carrying for a lot longer than you have."

I was moved to compassion as I thought of the people who I knew who had lived with a secret they could tell no one about for years, including my mum who had lived with her secret for over 36 years (that's how old I was at the time). Over the coming weeks, people began to open up about either their abuse, or they told me about someone they knew who had been abused.

You see, my mum had me at the tender age of 15 and for all these years, the secret surrounding the identity of my natural father seemed to be bigger than "who shot JR!"

And for her, the pain was intensified when my Grandmother (her mum), with whom I was raised, was brutally murdered in our home when I was 15. This was in 1982 and it wasn't until September 2003, just weeks before my own secret came out, that she was able to confirm that my biological father was the man responsible for murdering my Grandmother.

My Cause was Greater than My Shame

Just days before opening up to Chris, I recognized through a cousin that there was a pattern of abuse in our family. But it was the day that I looked at my daughter and felt such a deep love in my heart, that I pleaded with God and said, "No, not her." And although today I stand as a servant *of* God and a servant to people who have been suffering in silence for years, my first servant hood is *to* my little girl … my daughter Elodie.

> *…I recognized through a cousin that there was a pattern of abuse in our family.*

The conversation with my cousin increased the necessity of my cause and not only did I feel I held the key to breaking a generational curse of abuse in my family, I was motivated to put a stop to the enemy even trying to destroy her life through abuse – either physical or emotional.

The fear of Elodie taking the path that I'd taken was a real motivator for speaking out and I realize now that my cause was greater than my shame. But knowing that Jesus went to the cross to break all curses, and with my understanding of Romans 8, I have no doubt that the key to breaking all curses is walking a Spirit-filled life. I encourage you to read this chapter from both the King James and Amplified Versions of the Bible and I pray you'll be enlightened.

Chosen for a Purpose

In the months following, through my first encounter with the truth in my dining room, God took me on a journey that would lead to the establishment of my purpose.

My calling became very clear during the Blessed Women's Conference at our Church on the 22nd of November 2003. Lisa Bevere of *Messenger International* asked us to stand at different intervals to confirm our acceptance of certain tasks for God. I was compelled to stand after she asked "Who will write the books and the poems?" But as I stood there I said "God, how am I going to write 'that part' of my story?" 'That part,' relating to the abuse, since at that time, the story was not yet public.

Lisa Bevere then said, "You're asking God how you will write 'that part' of your story … He-will-tell-you-what-to-write."

All I could do was stand there and weep, and as I did, God showed me how He would use my story to set other women free. I had visions of women crying as I told my story—and them being set free from the bondage of their past.

My vision was confirmed the next day when one of my Pastors came looking for me after the Sunday morning service, to pray for me. He had no idea of the events of the previous evening but after he prayed, he said "God says 'what you've seen is nothing compared to what I'm going to do … I know your ability, now I just want your availability.'"

A week later, another Pastor said "God told me to 'tell Trish I am Sovereign and able, if she is willing.'"

This was the beginning of me establishing my ministry, *Women of Influence*—dedicated to helping women live on purpose and walk in God's fullness for their lives.

Your Turn …

You may be reading my story and thinking… "Trish you're brave, I could never tell," or "I did tell my husband and his reaction was quite the reverse to what you experienced."

Maybe your husband still holds your past against you and there may have been times when you've felt rejected, unloved and ashamed. But I want to remind you that God's Word says "There is therefore now no condemnation to them who are in Christ Jesus …" (Romans 8:1); and it's not up to your husband or anyone else to decide whether or not you're forgiven … But it is up to you to decide that you have been forgiven and to forgive yourself.

I can promise you that if you focus on God and walk in the light of His Spirit, your breakthrough will come… I can declare this on the authority of God's Word.

The first time I told my story publicly was at Church. I was so nervous. We sang Israel Houghton's song, a song I was hearing for the first time, *I lift up my hands standing unashamed* …

The fear left and I approached that platform with confidence, knowing that even if the whole congregation disapproved of my story, God approved of me.

God turned my 20-year-secret into His success story and now He wants to do the same for you.

⮚8⮘

PAULA BOND

Worthy of Love

Settling for crumbs in relationships is not what I imagined for myself. Deep down inside, it didn't ring true. 'Settling', however, became a part of my then, *perpetually broken-hearted* existence. For the longest time, dating was a nightmare. My inability to be honest with myself about some men's motives resulted in clouded judgment and misguided decisions.

Repeatedly, I found myself deeply disappointed after discovering that the guy I was dating had no intention of developing a serious relationship. My solution was to surrender to emotional compromise. I was simply afraid to face the fact that again my latest 'heartthrob' was only interested in one thing. At my lowest point I was no longer willing to justify the mismatched intentions. I'd finally run out of excuses to myself about why, once again, another relationship didn't work. Despite my desire for love, however, my actions exposed me as a young woman who believed herself to be *unworthy of love.*

Like many other little black girls growing up without fathers, I unwittingly had been searching for the love to replace what was missed so long ago. A father becomes the first and most profound standard a daughter refers to when she begins dating and eventually finds her husband.

My destiny with my husband was very far off. I was fine with that since I was now a high-fashion model gracing the runways of Paris, Rome, New York, Los Angeles and other places. It was an exciting life, no doubt. Paris was intoxicatingly beautiful, while Rome was soulful and passionate. During this life changing adventure God set in motion a work in me that remains in effect today. The Lord used strangers to begin revealing who I was supposed to be in Him. Social change was everywhere, the culture's standard of beauty was evolving at that time, and it was there in Europe where I would start the process of redefining my self-image.

Despite growing up with the limited perception of being a little black girl from the inner-city of Compton, California, as a young woman I was no longer offended by taunts about my full lips, nappy hair, or brown skin. The Europeans found my full lips sensual, my brown skin rich and glowing like tanned bronze and my hair was a crown of texture, able to be worked like a piece of art. A change of attitude changed my latitude.

Returning to America I worked as a TV Broadcaster. I also founded my own business teaching inner-city youth those 'life-changing,' esteem building skills I had absorbed like a sponge while in Europe. Professionally, things were good but my so-called 'love life' was a disaster.

I could not figure out why my otherwise glamorous life, was companionless. I became convinced that the *brotha's* were intimidated, after all I was 6 feet tall and had just returned from overseas. On the outside you saw a sister who kept her head up and handled her business, but on the inside a dark swirl of sadness was looming.

"God, I'm a good woman, where is my man?" I started to take it out on myself. "What's wrong with me, why am I not good enough?" My tears and pleading with the Lord began taking on a resentful tone, an angry edge. "Am I the object of a cruel joke, is this payback for sin?" I had no answers.

I got up every morning, did my hair and face, got dressed, and routinely masked the hurt that was slowly eroding the loveliness of my precious soul.

"Not again, Lord," as I'd find out that I'm one of the three women this guy is seeing. I'm feeling this downward spiral as depression is pulling up a seat and getting comfortable right alongside my life. Again my esteem is deflated, for not only is the man gone but a chunk of my self-confidence, a piece of my dignity and a slice of my self-respect also exited right behind him. All that lingered was his dysfunctional debris still entangled with my soul.

For ten more years I would date, but to no avail. Until one day. It felt as though I had strapped my emotions into a high powered race car. With every heart break the speed of that car would increase, faster and faster. . .fueled by disappointment and pain. . .and although the DEAD END is in sight, the racecar accelerates. . .I struggle to put on the brakes but too late . . .my emotions go *crashing*, hit hard!. . .slamming into a brick wall!

What I'd hit was my emotional bottom. That was it. No where else to turn, not another nightclub, not another concert, not another party. . . and even if my head could have tolerated just one more self-serving guy with his own agenda, there was no turning back, my heart was completely through, finished, kaput. I truly believed if I endured just one more heartache, the pain would have literally killed me.

"Dear God, please help me!" was all I could utter.

I'd been pushed over the edge into a pit where I had to look up to see bottom. I was depressed—but functional. It wasn't that my entire life was painful, I actually had a good life filled with family, great health, opportunity, and I knew the Lord. It was only love that was elusive.

Only love?. . . the most powerful component of our being. No wonder the pain cut so deep. I didn't want to die, nor was I willing to suffer any longer. My will was broken. I humbled myself and surrendered to God. "Not my way but thy way," was my prayer. Surrender was sweet!

A weight lifted, a burden relieved. I confessed to God my stubbornness in wanting relationships on my terms . . . never obeying His voice, only satisfying my every whim. God's word is clear, there is no confusion. Romans 12:1& 2 (NKJV) states, 1. "I beseech you therefore, brethren, by the mercies of God, that you present your bodies a living sacrifice, holy, acceptable to God, which is your reasonable service. 2. And do not be conformed to this world, but be transformed by the renewing of your mind, that you may prove what is that good and acceptable and perfect will of God." As children of God, our bodies belong to Him, which is number one. I belong to Him for His service. My mind needed to be renewed, and my obedience would render a testimony of His perfect will for my life. A change of attitude changed my latitude.

> *I confessed to God my stubbornness in wanting relationships on my terms . . . never obeying His voice, only satisfying my every whim.*

I did it! I took a break from dating. I got off the treadmill and made the Lord of Mercy my focus. I wanted to spend time with God, hear from Him, learn about Him and in the process learn about myself. Reordering my priorities was a great move. My depression began lifting and was replaced with prayer, meditation, bible study and a desire to learn what it means to be that special woman for the right man. Becoming a willing servant to our Loving God prepared me to submit to my future husband.

While dating, I had been so concerned about the man having a laundry list of perfect qualities, that I never put myself to the same litmus test. Studying the Word, reading books about women's issues, from both the Christian and secular perspectives really opened my eyes. I became so involved in my new habits that two years passed before I desired to date again. The Lord filled otherwise lonely times with friends, family and above all His Holy contentment. Isaiah 26:3A (KJV) reminds us, "Thou wilt keep him in perfect peace, whose mind is stayed on the..." Coming to understand that I am loved by God reconciled my heart. Learning of His unmatchable love blessed me with the gift of Fatherhood that I'd never received from my earthly father. Through the process of consecration to the Lord, I had finally become, *Worthy of Love.*

My very first date following two years of falling in love with Jesus was a blind date. It took prayerful consideration before I gave in but my sister assured me he was nice. Nice guy or not, I was only willing to commit an hour or so. No dinner, just refreshments and I was out of there. My sister and I arrived and went into the bar area of the restaurant. She saw someone at the bar and stepped away, leaving me in the middle of the room wondering if I had made a mistake and how I was going to get through this next hour. My sister soon motioned me over to meet her friend. . .wow!

He was handsome and had a warm, gracious manner. *Now why couldn't my blind date be like this guy?* Turns out, he was my blind date! I'm thinking, *ok so he's good looking, this is Hollywood where there's no shortage of good looking men, what about his character?* My sister's date arrived and the four of us found comfortable seating where we could talk. The evening actually went well and for the first time I began understanding what it meant to allow the All-Wise God guide my love life. A little over a year later my blind date named Gary would become my husband, Gary.

Gary and I spent our honeymoon on the island of Maui in Hawaii. Romantic... beautiful... serene... During our first morning walk on the beach Gary aggravated a groin muscle. At 6'2" tall and over 200 pounds this former professional Baseball player was over 45 years old yet still strong and fit. Back at home Gary's habit was to work out daily keeping himself in shape. So getting him to go to the doctor for the muscle strain was no easy task. As an athlete, Gary knew that a bit of pain was the price you paid for enjoying your sport. He was active in an over 40 baseball league and had won championships with his team.

He finally gave in and visited the doctor. When the hospital called back two weeks later asking him to do a follow-up appointment he took it in stride. Gary telephoned me at the conclusion of that second appointment and informed me that they were keeping him and I should grab a few of his things from the house before heading over to the hospital. Two months after we were married my husband was diagnosed with a terminal cancer.

The words from the doctor were unreal. Gary was given 18 months to live. God blessed him to live two and a half years. I had never known a greater love. No man ever treated me with such care and made me feel royal. We enjoyed those two and a half years. Each day was precious and sweet. I had never met a man with so many friends, sincere friends.

The funeral was attended by nearly 1,000 people. Gary was a remarkable human being, the definition of love. God knows I would not have traded the experience for all the money in the world.

Gary and I were absolutely clear that the Lord had chosen to use us. He used our love as a testimony of victory. Gary possessed the character and values I had been seeking in a man all my single years. When I was finally prepared, Sovereign God brought Gary to me, effortlessly. Almighty God didn't have to consult me on His plan; He simply performed His will through us, His willing vessels.

The Lord will deliver your blessings to you the moment you are truly prepared to receive. Get in His will, live a life of obedience. In it you will find true joy and peace. May the Lord bless you exceedingly, abundantly above anything that you can ask or think and may you always live a life *Worthy of Love.*

৵9৲

PAMELA KENNEBREW

Once Broken but Now Bold

"The wicked man flees though no one pursues, but the uncompromisingly righteous are as bold as a lion" (Proverbs 28:1 AMP).

Boldness is a by-product of righteousness. When we begin to walk in our righteousness we will become bold enough to possess those things that are ours in spite of any situation or circumstance. Boldness is a characteristic of a person with a Kingdom Mindset. When we are ruled by circumstances, our past or what may happen in the future, we become timid.

Timidity is anti-righteousness, anti-kingdom and anti-abundance. We have to be bold enough to receive and take possession of our *promise land*. Remember Joshua and Caleb? They didn't let the circumstances (the giants), the majority opinion (the 10 other leaders) or their past (40 years in the wilderness) stop them! They were bold.

Passivity is anti-righteousness and anti-kingdom. Passivity is a fear-based response to our external environment. Passivity is a deception of the enemy that allows us to accept his influence in our affairs. Matthew 11:12 states, "the kingdom of heaven suffers violence and the violent take it by force." In the Weust translation it reads "the kingdom of heaven is being taken by storm, and the strong and forceful ones claim it for themselves." We are to be strong and forceful when it comes to what belongs to us.

Boldness and Victory

When you understand who you are in Christ, you no longer live your life on the outside looking in or under the circumstances. When you know that you truly have nothing to lose because you have given it all to Jesus you have a 'holy boldness.'

You can stand in the face of adversity, sickness and disease and call those things that are not as though they were. You can be a 'Speaking Spirit' and not worry about what people may say. When you know that of yourself you are nothing and that your righteousness is in Christ you become bold. You can then go with strength and force, into the enemy's camp and take back what belongs to you. You can press into the throne, lay claim to the promises of God, and step back into the natural realm. You can speak the Word of God with a holy boldness that gives confident assurance that what you say will come to pass and what you do will succeed.

Boldness Through Brokenness

When we are able to confess our sins, trusting that God will honor His word and cleanse us from all unrighteousness we become bold.

"He who covers his sins will not prosper, but whoever confesses and forsakes them will have mercy" (Prov. 28:13).

Confession here doesn't mean tell it to our friends, it means confess to God (1 John 1:9). We can conclude from the verse in Proverbs that if we confess our sins we will prosper. In other words we will continue to make progress towards our purpose in God.

Be determined not to let your past mistakes dictate your future. I had to. A few years ago I experienced something that had the potential to ruin my reputation, my ministry and my future. A questionable business deal was made public. Like any negative news; it spread like wildfire. Some of my brothers and sisters in the Lord thought it was important to share the information with as many people as would listen. I was hurt, embarrassed and ashamed. In addition, I felt guilty because I had let so many people down; those who believed in me and supported me as well as those I had taught and ministered to.

My initial reaction was to run and hide. I had thoughts of moving out of town or doing whatever I could do to hide. The twin demons of guilt and shame together with their cousins, unforgiveness and bitterness were attempting to take over. All this took place two days before I was to begin teaching a course I designed called "Your Liberty in Christ." After a few words from people who truly knew and loved me; the scripture that I had in my heart started to spring up on the inside. I began to rehearse the Word on repentance and righteousness. I knew I had repented and it was time to walk in my righteousness. I walked into my class boldly and taught for the next 12 weeks like I had never taught before. Lives were changed and strongholds were broken.

It's easy to give up and feel unworthy, even to feel angry about how you are treated. I know I did, but I had to remember what God called me to do. I also had to remember it's not about me, and you have to remember it's not about you. It is about the lives that you are going to touch with your testimony.

I was broken. I had always relied on my reputation and image. What people thought of me was important, too important. But once I was shaken and brought low, there was nowhere to go but up!

This was a brokenness that led to boldness. The good thing about brokenness is that we can come to the Father in secret and confess our faults. We don't live in fear of being broken in front of others. When we allow God to deal with our issues, we don't have a fear of exposure.

God doesn't 'kiss and tell.' We experience true boldness when we don't have to worry about being exposed. When we keep things hidden we walk in fear of being exposed and we can't operate in boldness.

Boldness isn't arrogance. Be aware! There is a counterfeit boldness called arrogance. Some of us operate in this counterfeit boldness, which is actually a defense mechanism. Arrogance is derived from fear, guilt, shame and condemnation. When we are feeling guilty we use arrogance to cover up our true feelings. We will use whatever is in our hands or in our power as a 'fig leaf' to cover our nakedness and prevent exposure. For some it might be arrogance based on our education, for others it may be our status or position. Whatever it is we must recognize that it is a deception of the enemy. True boldness is born out of love, humility and submission to God's plan and purpose.

Boldness vs. Bragging

We are bold because of who we are in Him and apart from Him we are nothing and can do nothing. We must be bold in our speaking, boasting about Him, never bragging about ourselves. We must be careful to listen when others are bold and receive their boldness in love. It is important that we be obedient to the Word of God and trust Him. When we are concerned about what others think about our 'praise reports' for fear that they will accuse us of bragging or boasting, we need to check ourselves.

Boldness through Testimony

It is important that we share our testimony. God looks at the future while the enemy focuses on your past. By keeping things hidden we develop strongholds. These strongholds prevent us from moving forward in our purpose and plan. Remember the woman at the well. Once she received the revelation from Jesus, she went back to her own city and told the men there about Jesus. Let me say this, in the natural once you are taught a subject, the teacher gives an exam to see how much you have learned. The same is true in our spiritual life. Remember when Jesus admonished Peter, He said, "Satan desires to sift you like wheat, but I have prayed for you, and once you are converted, strengthen your brother."

Once you have come out of whatever situation or circumstance you are in, tell others. Your testimony will strengthen others. The Body of Christ would do well if we would become more transparent with the things that God has brought us through. We are in a war, and we have too many casualties. We know that the people outside the church are suffering because they are in the kingdom of darkness. However, there are people sitting next to you in the church who are experiencing the vicissitudes of life.

They have been praying to God to help them and you are their answer. When I offer to pray for or with someone, most of the time they are going through something that I have already experienced. If we would get our focus off of ourselves and turn our attention to 'one another' we would be sensitive to others and would know exactly what and when to share. It is so encouraging to be able to pray in faith and share with the other person how God moved on your behalf.

Our boldness must be greater than our circumstances. Every member of the Body of Christ is called to minister to others. We will be ridiculed and criticized by people from our past. However, it is important that we let others know about our failures, and how God was able to deliver us. Correctly responding to the tests and trials in our lives actually equips us for the future.

> *Correctly responding to the tests and trials in our lives actually equips us for the future.*

Sin consciousness will cause us to be defensive and self-conscious. Consciousness refers to your inner voice speaking to you regarding what is right and what is wrong. When you are sin-conscious, that voice is the enemy, when you are self-conscious it may be a combination of the enemy as well as your past. Defensiveness and self-consciousness will make us fearful to witness to others, particularly those we know. It will also inhibit our spiritual growth because we will be unable to evaluate constructive criticism and accept correction. When we lack boldness we fail to walk in abundance because we can't see the richness of the 'teachable' moments around us. Don't let your boldness slip because you feel guilty or condemned.

50

"By this we shall come to know (perceive, recognize, and understand) that we are of the Truth, and can reassure (quiet, conciliate, and pacify) our hearts in His presence, whenever our heart in (tormenting) self-accusation make us feel guilty and condemn us. And, beloved, if our consciences (our hearts) do not accuse us (if they do not make us feel guilty and condemn), we have confidence (complete assurance and boldness) before God" (1 John 3:19,21).

We have a high priest, Jesus the Son of God, and because of Him and Him alone we can come boldly to the Father. It is the Blood of Jesus that took away our sin (our sin nature) and continually cleanses us of our sins when we repent.

As you are reading this book, you may be identifying with the situations presented here. But you must go beyond just identification. You must truly repent, not feel sorry for yourself, but repent and receive the gift of righteousness through faith in Jesus and the power of His Blood to cleanse and forgive. Many of us live defeated lives because we have faith in our own righteousness rather than the righteousness of God. In some cases we feel guilty and hang on to past sins and un-surrendered areas in our lives instead of surrendering them to Jesus. Guilt and condemnation keep us in the outer court where we can sing and profess our love to God, but we can't go into the throne. Because of sin consciousness, we don't feel worthy to come boldly.

When you first come to Jesus you acknowledge you are a sinner and accept His work on Calvary. From that point on Jesus is your High Priest and advocate or lawyer. Just like any lawyer, Jesus speaks for you. You have power of attorney to use His Name.

Jesus said to the Father, "I know you hear me and you always hear me." Once you gain boldness through a redemptive revelation of righteousness, you can say the same thing. You have confidence and boldness in your prayer life. You come boldly to the throne of God and you walk in victory in every area of your life.

❧10❦

NICOLLA RENEE'

Faithful in a Very Little

"**G**et rid of them."
I heard these words in my spirit and I was taken aback. What? I could hardly believe what I was hearing, but it came again very calmly and clearly, "Get rid of them." God was admonishing me to get rid of—of all things—books.

Because I was committed to living a godly lifestyle, I had no problem refraining from things like, alcohol, smoking, fornication...you know, the "biggies" that can separate us from God, frustrate our efforts to bear fruit in our lives and enjoy His promises.

I thought I was doing well in my walk with the Lord, so this admonishment came as quite a surprise; especially over something so small and seemingly insignificant.
"Get rid of them."

Without even scanning my bookshelf, I knew precisely which books the Lord was referring to. I could have walked by and easily pulled each specific title off the shelf; and yet I wondered, what was wrong? Why was God speaking to me about these books?

Being an avid reader, over the years I had collected probably hundreds of books, primarily fiction. During high school and college, my weekend outlet to unwind from the rigors of study was to devour magazines and escape into the latest bestselling paperback novels—everything from mysteries to romances to sci-fi. I had shelves full of books, and ultimately boxes full when I ran out of shelf space.

My books were like familiar friends which I meticulously cared for. I didn't mark them, nor fold back pages. I did not bend the binding back and create creases in the spine. I didn't even like to leave finger smudges on the covers. I could read a book from cover to cover and leave it looking like brand new.

I was such a good steward over my books that I remained puzzled over God's gentle but constant insistence, "Get rid of them."

Okay, I would get rid of them, but first I wanted to understand why. As I pulled the books in question off the shelf and stacked them in a corner, I said, "Okay Lord, I'm taking them down now." He repeated His refrain, "Get rid of them." It felt as though God owed me some sort of explanation for all this; yet none came.

After a little more time, I boxed the offending titles and said, "Okay Lord, they are boxed and right by the door on their way out." His simple response, "Get rid of them."

His voice never got loud, angry, impatient or critical; yet it also never wavered. In a last ditch effort to understand just why these books were so important to God, I inquired, "Well Lord, they are in such perfect condition, can't I at least donate them?" He responded, "If they are not good for you to keep, what makes them good for someone else?"

I finally conceded, grabbed the boxes and tossed them out into the dumpster. As they slipped into the dark bin, a sharp light of awareness penetrated my consciousness. It's not that the books were so important to God...it's that they were too important to me!!

Something "so small and seemingly insignificant" actually represented a great and very significant area in my life where my wrong relationship with things, such as the books, caused me to hesitate in obeying God's voice. It may have seemed small to me, but God was showing me that by idolizing books I was not quick to obey His directive—and that was a big problem. He is to come first—there should be nothing in my life that prevents me from immediately obeying His voice, for lack of obedience, and even delayed obedience, is sin.

The big issue here was that my wrong relationship with books caused me to hesitate in immediately heeding God's word when He told me to get rid of the books. I was humbled...I was convicted...I was grateful. Repentant, I thanked God for revealing that area of my life which I had not completely submitted to His authority. I looked for other areas where I might have been unknowingly in wrong relationship with things— music, clothes, shoes, food, money, people. There were no further admonishments, but I had learned a valuable lesson about the importance of checking to ensure that my relationship with things did not supersede my relationship with God.

When I obeyed God in getting rid of the books, I experienced increased peace and joy. I had yielded to God's authority, submitted to His control and showed myself that I was willing to follow Him—in everything. Yet I realize yielding is a continual process—a constant vigil. God will work with us on even the seemingly small details in our lives where we need to grow and change to be in right relationship with Him.

While I understand that books in general were not the problem, correcting the importance I had placed on them made me realize that the kinds of books I chose and what they caused me to meditate on was worth analyzing. I believe God wanted me to be more discerning in my book selections and rather than seek a diet of constant entertainment and escape, I needed to shift my focus to more edifying and empowering selections.

Once I submitted this area to God's authority, my reading interests changed dramatically. I desired to read for edification, especially spiritual edification, and focused on subjects that honored Him. I no longer enjoyed reading books or magazines that were not in line with God's Word; I craved information that would help me live better and achieve abundance.

Ultimately, my obedience made room for the blessing God intended for me all along. He wasn't trying to deprive me or take something away from me; He was asking me to make room for a greater blessing. After my becoming faithful in a very little, the Lord blessed me with the vision to launch a publishing company to publish a women's magazine, *Inspired Living*, as well as inspiring books and other spiritually edifying products.

> **Ultimately, my obedience made room for the blessing God intended for me all along.**

In the Parable of the Minas found in Luke 19, the wealthy nobleman gave ten of his servants money to engage in business while he was away. Upon his return he called his servants to him to see what they had earned. The first servant had earned ten minas prompting the nobleman to say, "Well done, good servant; because you were faithful in a very little, have authority over ten cities" (Luke 19:17).

When we trust and obey God and believe that what He has for us is better than what we are holding onto, He rewards our faithfulness. For me it was books, for you it might be your relationship with money, a mate, a job, food, people, etc. Are you willing to heed God's voice and do what He is telling you to do in your life, no matter how seemingly insignificant? Like the good servant, be faithful in a very little and God will promote you to the greater blessings He has planned for you.

∻11∻

NICOLE CLEVELAND

My Spiritual Resume

O ne of the songs that ministered to me in the midst of my storm was "Because Of Who You Are." The way Martha Munizzi sang the lyrics helped soothe the pain. Lying on the floor all alone on that summer evening I could feel the tears welling up in my eyes, my heart pounded as if to jump out of my chest. Anxiety attacks were normal at this point; they would visit me at least once a day. Then that queasy feeling would rise in my stomach as if I had to vomit.

"Abandoned" was the term the courts gave to my situation. But how could this have happened? We attended church regularly. He was a minister and our family was very active in the church.

He was from a good family, with two parents at home, and had been raised in the church from the time he was a baby. Evangelists, Preachers, Missionaries, Pastors and Bishops were the roles in his family. He knew right from wrong. He knew the consequences. That's one of the commandments, "Thou shall not commit adultery." If anyone was to sway it should have been me.

Church was not part of the routine when a teenaged single mother was raising me. The fear of God was not instilled in me. Church was not mandatory on Easter, Mother's Day, or even Christmas. Christmas was all about toys in our home, not Christ.

My husband left me in 2004.

Daily I searched my mind looking for the signs that I had failed to notice and it was pure torment; a slow agonizing self-torment similar to needles being repeatedly stuck in my soul.

Was my skin complexion too dark? Did I put on too many pounds after the kids? Did I not clean enough? Cook enough? Was I at the office too many hours? Did I not give him enough sex? Was I at church too much? I call these my "shoulda, coulda, woulda" moments.

Our third child was born on April 24, 2004. Four days later my husband announced his departure. *What in the world! Has he lost his mind?* My body, mind and spirit were not up for it at that time. I felt sensitive, vulnerable, unguarded, and defenseless.

"For we wrestle not against flesh and blood, but against principalities, against powers, against the rulers of the darkness of this world, against spiritual wickedness in high places" (Ephesians 6:12 KJV).

"Cry, cry, cry, that's all you do Nicole," he would tease. "Get over it. I don't want you anymore, we are done."

He was right. In the beginning all I would do is cry. From the time I woke up to the time I went to bed. At that time his parents stayed with us to help me with the kids so I had some peace— just a little. The Lord truly blessed me with a good mother and father-in-law. My mother-in-law is one of those saved, sanctified COGIC mothers, who stand on the word and the word only. Even in my husband's mess they never took up for him like some parents do.

I can remember my mother-in-law saying, "If that boy makes his bed in hell that's where he's gonna lay. I ain't taking up for him. Right is right and wrong is still wrong," she would say. "What kind of mother would I be if I took up for his mess?"

But so many parents do it.

"Love the person, hate the sin..."She would remind me. That was a tough pill for me to swallow. I wanted revenge. I wanted him to pay for my tears, my pain, and the pain he took my kids through when he walked away.

My six year old would cry herself to sleep because she wanted her daddy. My 14 year old thought the church was a hoax. "How could daddy be a minister in the church and then leave his family and not care?" he would ask. How could I answer a boy being raised in the church with the teachings that fornication was wrong, adultery was wrong, but his dad is living across town with another woman?

> *"Yeah right, everybody blames everything on the devil. He left because he wanted to."*

"It's the devil; the enemy," I would tell him.

"Yeah right, everybody blames everything on the devil. He left because he wanted to."

And he was right. We are given choices and he made the choice to leave.

I could write this story and say I just wanted my husband to come to his senses and wake up. But that would be a lie. At one point I wanted him dead so that I could collect social security benefits. How crazy was that?

Love the person; hate the sin.

The Masquerade

I became a professional mask wearer. Not many people outside of my circle and church family knew what was going on. Continuing with my daily routine was a job in itself. At work I would be in the middle of a meeting and would have to excuse myself to go to the ladies room where I would break down in silence. Covering my mouth so no one would know I was crying, trying to hold my breath to keep it in. This scene would take place at least once a day. It would end with cold water being splashed on my face.

After work in the car I would keep the windows up and just scream, cry and thank God that I made it through work another day. I had to keep it together. My job was my bread and butter. I was a single parent now. My husband had decided he was not helping with anything. His money was his money. So I had to turn the law on him.

Child support, spousal support, custody of the kids; we went through it all. Summons after summons was not a joyous ride. I can remember one court appearance we had to go to for spousal support. He had asked if he could ride with me because he didn't have a car. I kept our vehicle since I had the children. He opened the car door, sat down and turned to look at me and I was disgusted. I wanted to vomit. When he turned towards me I noticed several passion marks on his face and neck. They were very visible. I would even say they were intentional, and they were meant to be seen. He knew he was coming to court the next day so he wanted to show me that he was getting it on.

This was a new level of pain that actually made me nauseous. I told him to exit my vehicle. I was trying so badly to keep it together because I had come to realize that when I cried around him, he only tormented me more. It gave him, the enemy, power. He wanted me to lose my mind.

"For we wrestle not against flesh and blood, but against principalities, against powers, against the rulers of the darkness of this world, against spiritual wickedness in high places" Ephesians 6:12 (KJV).

57

But I wanted so badly to cry out, "Why are you doing this to me?" But I didn't. I just thought, "Lord give me strength to hold back the tears until he is out of my presence."

Of course I was awarded the spousal support. Why would he come to court and claim he was not sleeping with someone but have obvious passion marks on his face and neck? The enemy had him deceived.

After I got done with him his take-home pay was about $300 every two weeks. Since he wanted to play, he was going to pay. But truthfully, I just wanted my husband back. At one point I was so desperate that I was going to allow the affair. "Women do it all the time," I reasoned. They know about the mistress but never say anything. It's just something silent that's never discussed. One older woman told me that her husband had an affair with the woman on the next street and the only time he made love to her was when the other woman was on her period. She just accepted it because he was a good provider. I'm sorry. I couldn't do it. I had too much respect for myself and I had a 14 year old son who I did not want thinking that was the way a woman should be treated.

After the court room appearance the Lord showed me that this thing was so much bigger than me. I was to intercede on behalf of my husband—fasting and praying was to be my regular actions until he came to himself. You see, on that day of court I realized that the enemy had my husband as a puppet.

Years ago, when we first got married, my husband had my name tattooed on his arm. Well, after a few months he had his other woman's name tattooed on his other arm. So he was walking around with my name on one arm and her name on another arm. He was in complete confusion. The enemy had set a trap for him and he had fallen.

"A double minded man is unstable in all his ways" (James 1:8 KJV).

I loved my husband and didn't want him to die in his sin and go to hell. He was the father of my children, so I took Nicole and her fleshy feelings out of the situation, and began seeing him only as God saw him. This was extremely hard but if I could witness and love my co-workers and strangers on the street why couldn't I do the same for my husband?

Love the person; hate the sin.

In January 2005 during my morning prayer, the Holy Spirit told me to call my husband on his job and tell him, "Enough is enough, it's time to come home." For a brief moment I thought it was the enemy and not the Lord because Nicole did not want to call him or tell him anything. I wrestled with this because he was so mean to me and had hurt me so badly.

Hadn't he come home three times previously and left each time? Didn't he call me a few weeks ago to tell me that the girl was pregnant? I told him I would never allow him back in our home if he got her pregnant. I have learned never to say what you won't do.

I can remember telling my mother-in-law that the chapter in my life with her son was closed. And she asked me with her sanctified voice, "Did God say it was closed?"

But I heard it again and I knew it was the Lord. Being obedient I made the call against Nicole's fleshy feelings, and my husband came back two hours later.

My Resume

Three years ago I truly thought I would lose my mind. I wrestled against suicidal thoughts, lost 25 lbs, had self-esteem issues, battled insomnia and questioned God as to why this would happen to me. Now I know that God chose me to endure, understanding that everybody could not have gone through what I had to go through.

You see I left out that when he and the girl moved—they moved right up the street from us, and our home was almost in foreclosure. So many things took place all due to a bad choice that could never be overturned.

My home budget was short almost $1000 every month because of his bad choices. So when the telephone was disconnected, the electricity was shut off, and there was no heat, the peace I had (and still have) is credited to God. My paycheck had to carry the entire household for months because when my husband returned, he owed everybody—and they wanted their money.

She had the baby. One day when I came home from work there was a summons on my door. The summons was for child support for a baby boy named after my husband. At that exact moment I thought I would pass out.

Did it hurt, oh yes… it was like the cycle was starting all over again. But this time I started with a peace. God has given me a spiritual resume and I refuse to allow anyone or anything to delete any section that God has carried me through.

When situations arise now, and they do, I pull out my spiritual resume. I scan the sections and say to myself, "He took me through that period in my life and I know he will take me through this." Do you have a spiritual resume? I do.

๕12๕

MARILYN HILTON

Singing to the God of Your Life

"By day the Lord directs his love, at night his song is with me— a prayer to the God of my life" (Psalm 42:8 NIV).

Everyone has a song—a story in a language deeper, wider, and richer than words alone can tell. My song starts with a frightening phone call I received several years ago, one that would change my life. The caller was a surgeon who had performed a biopsy on me a week before, and what he told me was that it appeared I had cancer.

Anyone who has heard those words spoken over the phone or in the doctor's office knows the mental and physical process that takes place following. First, you feel disconnected; we're talking about someone else here. Second, as the reality sets in, your mind freezes and you forget how to do the simplest things, like close up your purse or find your keys or drive home. Then, you want to run away—to any place but where you are—but then you realize that no matter where you go, what you're trying to escape will still be with you. I went through all these stages, and more, in the first hour after I received the phone call.

At the time, my husband and I had two beautiful little girls, both under three years old, who needed both of their parents. That I, a wife and a mother of two babies could receive such bad news seemed both unreal and unjust.

Also during that time, my husband and I had been trying to have a third child, and after several months of working unsuccessfully with an infertility specialist, we'd given up. But when I received my news, I realized that my inability to conceive had been a blessing. If I'd been pregnant at the time, one way or another, I would have had to make some very difficult, painful decisions that would have affected my life and the

60

lives of my husband, two daughters, and the child I would be carrying. Still, giving up the dream of that third child and forever having to look at the empty place at the table broke my heart.

The first step toward getting an accurate diagnosis and prognosis was more tests and then surgery. As the hours and then days wore on while test results were coming back and the surgery was to be scheduled, I found myself praying to a God with whom I had lost touch over the years. Even then, this was a God of whom I'd only asked favors and good outcomes. Although I'd been raised in the church, I didn't know God as my Creator or Jesus as Lord and Savior. I'd been a good person and obeyed rules and was

> *Although I'd been raised in the church, I didn't know God as my Creator or Jesus as Lord and Savior.*

kind to others, and so it seemed reasonable that God should answer my desperate prayers now, at a time when my mortality wasn't some faraway concept but was staring me squarely in the eyes, deeper and deeper as the hours wore on.

As we waited, and as I tried to keep life normal for me, my husband, and our two sweet girls, I said many prayers, which sounded like this: "Don't let it be this," and "Don't let it be that," and "Make the trees sway if I'm going to get through this." But those prayers didn't seem to work. I didn't feel any sense of relief or tap on the shoulder or burning sensation in my body, and I didn't see the trees sway or the sky turn green. Instead, with every doctor visit, every phone call, and every new test, the news just got worse.

But I kept on praying anyway, sure that if I said the right words or had the proper attitude, I'd hit the bull's-eye, and God would tell me He heard me and He was fixing my problem.

Then, on the morning of my surgery, after my husband prayed for me in our car in the hospital parking lot, and after I sat in a curtained-off cubicle with a nurse who asked me lots of questions and patted me on the shoulder sympathetically, and after I changed into a gown and lay on the gurney that would take me to the operating room, I closed my eyes.

Lying there, I saw everything I lived for and loved fall away: my husband, my daughters, my home, my job, my dreams, my health, and even my life. I realized that everything precious to me, which I clung to, could be taken from me as quickly as a pulse. Everything in this life, I realized, was fleeting, fragile, and temporary.

Suddenly, I knew the prayer that I should have been praying all along. Before the sedative that would put me to sleep could take effect, I said one last prayer. "Lord," I said, "whatever happens to me—whether I die on the operating table or wake up, or whether the final news is good or bad—please don't leave me. I can stand anything as long as I know You are with me."

I knew it was the prayer He'd been waiting for, because immediately I was filled with peace and—yes—joy. And I knew that nothing could hurt me as long as He was with me. As those dear but fleeting aspects of my world grew dim and fell away, the power, presence, and truth of God grew stronger and brighter. I knew that, no matter what happened, He would always be right there at my side. He was the only true thing I could count on. And He would never leave me, no matter what happened.

After the surgery, my prognosis was very good—thankfully. But, I knew that even if the news hadn't been good, the *real* news was still excellent. God would always be with me—even as He ushers me into the real life He has planned. How tragic it would have been if, healthy or otherwise, I had lived the rest of my life without learning that truth.

They say that there are no atheists in the foxhole and, clichéd as it may sound, this was true in my case. I saw my crisis as God's challenge to me. He was asking, "Now, what direction are you going to take? What do you plan to do with what you've learned?"

My response to God, whose truth and character I saw revealed so clearly and powerfully that I could not deny Him, was to offer the rest of my life to Him. The first thing was, of course, to make up for all the lost years and get to know Him better—Him, Almighty God, not the God of convenience I'd created in my mind.

That gift of understanding God's character alone was abundant enough, but God didn't stop there. He never stops where we do. Six months later I discovered by complete surprise that I was pregnant. Medically and logistically, the pregnancy should have been impossible. But I knew my beautiful boy was my Heavenly Father's special gift to me—the one I never expected.

"Know how much I love you," I heard Him say.

God sang to me my son. And in return, I sing this song to Him—my story of His profound love.

It's not easy—in fact, it's downright impossible to sing when our world is crumbling around us. When singing is the last thing you want to do, remember that our God is the one true thing in life—the only thing we can count on. Sometimes, though He'll take what seems to be drastic and terrifying measures to make us understand that, He will never abandon us. His song is with you, always and forever.

❧13❧

REBEKAH L. PIERCE

When the Odds Are Stacked Against You

I have definitely defied the odds and can speak from experience that "it's not about where you've been, but where you're going!" Growing up poor in Stockton, CA with limited resources, I fought hard for the opportunity to attend college and become somebody. I barely escaped the hands of death at the age of 18 when I attempted to take my own life to flee the harsh road and lies that were whispered into my spirit about my self-worth. But my mother's hard work and struggle to give my siblings and me better opportunities superseded those lies and gave me the strength to press on and become the woman I am today.

As an African-American military veteran and prevailing entrepreneur, I know that my purpose is to give a voice to women from all walks of life through the pages of my publication, *Average Girl Magazine*, and through the sharing of my story. I know that stepping out on faith when the odds are stacked against me has set me on a path that only God knew I could handle.

Now, don't get me wrong, I have had many days that every first stage entrepreneur who steps out on faith dreads: hearing that your idea is great, but because you have no resources (i.e., money), you'll never make it happen. In the past four years, I have heard every excuse from high powered business persons to those just starting that there's no way I will be able to grow this company because I don't have those thousands of dollars behind me. If I had a quarter for every time I heard that, I'd be able to buy a condominium...in the Hamptons.

So, when does one "give up?" Or in business jargon, "when do you start executing your exit strategy?" When every door closes in your face? When you turn off your cell phone to avoid the bill collectors? When your spouse starts to give you that "this isn't working" look? When you run out of faith? My entire life has been about battling the odds and taking the road least traveled. There's something in me that just has to march to a different drum beat.

The day that I tried to take my life was the actual beginning of my journey through faith. I let my doubt about who I was and what I could be cloud my vision and distort my faith. As I swallowed those pills, though, something whispered to my spirit that I was worthy…that my family needed me more than I knew. God told me that I would always be somebody to Him…if only I would believe and have faith. He told me that He had a gift in me that needed to come out…if only I would believe. I have been moving and walking in faith since that day.

> **The day that I tried to take my life was the actual beginning of my journey through faith.**

I will admit, though, that there are days when I do feel like giving up on everything. What human being doesn't? I think aloud everyday about giving up this "foolish" idea of entrepreneurship and going back to work for someone else because at least then I'd have a steady paycheck, health insurance and the coveted 401 (k). But then my spirit would die and that scares me more than not having a paycheck. Sometimes, I think that I must be an alien. *Why else would I risk my security to save my spirit?*

This past Christmas, I was sitting in a Christmas play called "The Gift" when I heard a character say something that gave me an "Ah hah!" moment. The character said: "God's gift to you is potential. Your gift to God is what you do with that potential." How profound for me that statement was because what I realized was that my potential is my purpose, and my purpose is my gift to God; but only when I move in it. The blessings don't come until you MOVE.

One of my favorite inspirational quotes is by Maya Angelou: "I can be changed by what happens to me. I *refuse* to be *reduced* by it." What this means to me is that no matter what happens with my business or in my life's purposeful journey, I will not let it change the essence that is me. I am a child of God and He has given me my purpose…no matter the odds, I have to fulfill it. I can see it, feel it, touch it and even smell it. That's purpose!

So what's yours? What steps have you taken to pursue your purpose? There's an ancient Chinese proverb that says: "Ambition knows no obstacles." I think this moment is the best time to be ambitious and purposeful. Know that God has blessed you with potential, purpose—a gift. Use your faith to guide and move you towards fulfilling your purpose.

Know that this is the year of your completion—whatever that may be for you. Believe in your gift; work on your gift; and share your gift. But more importantly, write it down on a piece of paper and carry it with you in your wallet or purse, and when you have a moment when you feel as if the world is coming down on you, and it will because that is life, take it out and repeat it to yourself until you feel calm enough to put it away again and go on with your day.

Remember! Life isn't easy. If it were, we wouldn't have the chance to show God what we can do with His gift to us. Your purpose is waiting for you. Get started on your purpose plan today and don't let your past be the roadblock to your purpose-driven life. MOVE! It's time to step out on faith.

≈14≈

KAREN HUDSON

Peace through Adversity

"I will not leave you as orphans; I will come to you" (John 14:18).

Abuse, a crippling surgery, divorce, and breast cancer. I could have handled any of these with time to heal between each, but I didn't have that luxury. It was more than I could bear. I was raised as a Christian, my family always trusting our Lord. However, I have to admit by the time I got to breast cancer, I was questioning God. I have always been told that God would not put on you more than you could handle. Apparently, He didn't know me very well.

I quit going to church and started to wallow in this deep hole of self pity. It seemed as though everyone else was having a wonderful life, why not me? What did I do to deserve this? I tried to live my life right, I just didn't understand. During this time of trying to turn away from God I have to admit that I still prayed. But my prayers were very angry. I yelled at God, telling Him I couldn't do this.

As I look back I realize that God was there, just not the way I wanted Him to be. I wanted Him to make it go away; to wake up feeling good, the way I thought everyone else did. I could not remember a time as an adult when my life was calm. I just wanted a little time that I could feel what I assumed was normal.

Breast cancer: Seven months after my foot surgery, I had an appointment for my yearly gynecological exam. I was not worried that something would be wrong; I was just dreading the process. A few days later I received a call from the nurse stating the doctor had found a lump and wanted me to have a biopsy. I had the biopsy done and within days I received the dreaded call.

"Karen, our tests indicate that the lump is cancer. You need to make an appointment with a surgeon as soon as possible."

I cried for several days, then decided it was time to act. I made an appointment with a surgeon in the area. He said he would remove the lump, some of the surrounding tissue, and then put me through radiation. Because I had trusted a doctor that ended up crippling me, I was apprehensive. So, I went to see another surgeon. He told me almost the same thing, with just a few differences. Neither of these doctors took time to explain what was happening to me. I was terrified. I decided that I needed to talk to someone else. I located the name of the director of our Breast Cancer Center and set up an appointment to talk to her. Armed with my biopsy report, a pad and pencil, I went to see her. She was wonderful. She looked at my report, and then went on to thoroughly explain what it meant. She also gave me details of my options, giving me the names of two surgeons out of town who she knew had dealt with a lot of breast cancer cases. I chose one located in Louisville, Kentucky because the drive would not be difficult. She contacted the physician and set up an appointment for me.

Within 20 minutes, the surgeon in Louisville had my respect and my faith in him. He took a lot of time explaining breast cancer. He gave me details on my options. He wanted me to also speak to a plastic surgeon before making my final decision. He called one of the plastic surgeons that he recommended, located in the same building, to see if it would be possible to get me in while I was in town. As it happened, this surgeon was just coming out of surgery and agreed to see me immediately.

Entering the examining room in his surgery scrubs, Dr. D immediately put me at ease. He introduced himself, examined me, and looked at my records which I carried down with me to his office. He was gentle, kind, and compassionate. He spent 30 minutes with me, giving me information and making me feel special. Having gone through a divorce during the aftermath of my foot surgery, I had very low self esteem. He bolstered it a little, all the while still maintaining his professional manner. I knew if I decided to have a bi-lateral mastectomy, which was the recommendation of the cancer surgeon I had just talked to, this man would be my plastic surgeon. I later found out that his aunt had died from breast cancer and he promised her that he would always do everything he could for anyone with this horrible disease. He was also a Christian.

Can you see where God was working in my life? I did not, not until later. He was leading me to all of the right people. I started to feel a sense of strength that would allow me to do what I needed. I went to the library and checked out several books. I read all of them, making notes of things that I felt applied to me. I talked to a friend who had been through breast cancer a couple of years before. After taking in all I could, I made my decision; I would have the bi-lateral mastectomy and breast reconstruction. I met with each of the doctors in Louisville one more time before the surgery date. I had no misgivings at all. I knew this was the right thing to do.

One of the things that did concern me was that most of my family was away from me. My son, a teenager, was embarrassed to talk to me about the breast cancer. I understood, but I needed him desperately. One of my sisters did live nearby and offered to take me to Louisville for my surgeries and any follow-up appointments. Her work schedule allowed her some flexibility. For this I will be eternally grateful. She was my guardian angel, during my surgery, my reconstruction, and my long recovery.

> *I was still angry at God. Now I am angry at myself for not trusting in Him.*

I had my surgery and all went well. I was still angry at God. Now I am angry at myself for not trusting in Him.

During my recovery, a last minute cancellation had opened up a spot for another person to attend Tres Dias, a religious weekend retreat. My sister called me, asking if I wanted to go. Reminding her that I had to do therapy several times a day, and would have to leave in the middle of some of the lectures, I accepted.

The theme of our weekend was "Peace through the Holy Spirit." Yes, God was working in my life. First the right contacts, now this. Everyone I met at Tres Dias was so very loving and supportive. I learned a lot during my spirit-filled weekend. It was the most wonderful time I have ever been through. God's love was abundant each and every minute. I made many new Christian friends, each giving me a special feeling and a little more strength to deal with my cancer. As I was healing on the outside, God was healing me on the inside. I literally found peace through the Holy Spirit.

❧15❧

CRISSY SANDERS

It May Take Awhile, But Persevere

Galatians 6:9 *"Let us not become weary in doing good, for at the proper time we will reap a harvest if we do not give up."*

It takes about six years for one nice sized pearl to be fashioned. Imagine how much work it is for oysters to create an entire strand of pearls that a person wears around their neck.

If you desire to generate pearls in your era you are going to have to enroll for the marathon and forget about any sprinting. To successfully complete a marathon, individuals train for elongated periods of time. In life, we have got to take the marathon approach in order to be prepared for where God is taking us in the future.

It is in this lengthy course of action that large amounts of people spiral out of control in discouragement. They abandon the assignment that God has prearranged for them because they have a sprint mentality and easily grow weary in well doing.

You don't have to yield to this tactic of the devil. I do not know precisely what God has for you. I am not familiar with the breakthrough that you need in your life or your ministry. But I do know from experience that it is worth every fragment of the waiting time. Each period of the interval becomes a block that God uses to build upon in order to advance you for His ultimate purpose.

It's Okay If You Don't Understand, You Must Still Trust Him

I have a son who is currently 15 years old. While I was in my first trimester of pregnancy with him, my husband lost his job of many years. We were not in the ministry at the time and we had to stretch our finances to inconceivable lengths. He lost his job because his supervisor blamed theft on him. Many months after he was dismissed, the company found out that it was my husband's supervisor who was the true thief.

We were Christians at the time. We were faithful to God in our finances and our witness. So, here I was pregnant and we had no insurance and we had no money. There were many days that there wasn't even food in our cabinets. We were surviving off of the church food pantry which consisted of stale crackers and canned meat. Because we didn't have the money to pay our rent we were forced to live with my in-laws. We could not understand why God was allowing it to happen. My husband spent hours and hours each week seeking employment. This was in 1991, and jobs were few and far between in our region of the country.

We were faithful to God despite not comprehending why we were enduring such circumstances. There were days that we wondered if that season would ever pass.

Now, 15 years later, we can look back and understand why these conditions had to take place in our lives. God permitted those struggles to prepare us for the countless individuals that we would have to counsel and guide with their finances. God taught us how to trust in Him and not our checkbook. This experience equipped us to pastor people who have been treated unfairly and falsely accused. God gave us the opportunity to produce a pearl that even today we pull out and appreciate the beauty of.

> *God taught us how to trust in Him and not our checkbook.*

We persisted despite pain. We walked when we desired to weep. We praised when we felt like pouting and in our due season we are reaping the harvest that God promised us way back then.

God yearns to do this very same thing in your life. But, you must wait for the appointed time.

A Lesson From an Invalid

In John 5 there is an account of a man at the pool of Bethesda who was an invalid. This man was laying at Bethesda for 38 years waiting for his miracle.

The bible teaches us that at certain times the water at the pool of Bethesda stirred. The first one to get into the pool received a healing from their disease. After all of these years, this invalid's hope was deferred.

The word Bethesda means House of Mercy and Place of Outpouring. He was at the location of mercy and outpouring, yet he had received none of these.

Thirty eight years of anticipation with no improvement had to be disheartening. Yet, he stayed put. He was an invalid which means that he couldn't care for himself.

There are a lot of 'invalid' Christians in the church world. Folks who should be moving forward, but instead they are frail and spiritually anemic. Today, people surrender to their struggle and leave Bethesda instead of remaining. The recompense, conversely only comes to the ones who persist despite any amount of inconvenience.

There he was in John 5:6 doing the same thing that he had been doing all of those other days, months and years. The difference about this day however was that Jesus was about to arrive at this place and do some stirring Himself.

When Jesus appeared at the pool, He saw that this individual had been in this condition for 38 years. Our loving Savior was moved with compassion, and asked him if he wanted to get well.

I imagine that when first spoken to, this hurting man must have thought to himself numerous different things. Maybe he wondered why anyone was even speaking to him. He might have reflected to himself that it was pretty obvious that he wanted to get well. I am convinced that he had to feel like no one was sensitive about his condition. Each person at this natural Bethesda was only there for themselves.

It is in these situations that we tend to feel sorry for ourselves. That day, when he gazed at the one who was requesting a response, he wasn't just glancing into the eyes of another hurting human being. He was fixing his eyes on the supernatural Bethesda. The only one who could speak a single word and create worlds. This was the only begotten Son of God who is a miracle manufacturer.

The natural Bethesda is a place that many of us have found ourselves at. It is a position that we often place ourselves in while trying to make things happen on our own time scale.

The Supernatural Bethesda, on the other hand, is the living, breathing, way maker that always brings about a harvest in its due season. There is a difference between us and this invalid in John 5. He never had the opportunity, prior to this day, to encounter the Supernatural Bethesda; while we have countless opportunities daily to converse with the architect of our souls. This dispirited man was about to receive what he had been waiting for all of those years. He answered the Master, and was told to pick up his mat and walk.

Now, imagine with me for a moment, what this man must have thought. He surely contemplated to himself, "I have been laying here all of these years in pain and agony, and this man shows up today and tells me to pick up my mat and walk." One thing is certain, he didn't argue with Jesus. The Scripture says that this man did exactly as he was told to do.

With access 24/7 to the Supernatural Bethesda, you have hope and triumph awaiting you. Don't be downcast because of a temporary setback. Pick yourself up and walk on in Jesus name!

Two Steps to Aim for Daily in Order to Be a Pearl Creator.
1. Dream

To dream is to hope. (Isaiah 40:31) "Those who hope in the Lord will renew their strength, they will soar on wings like eagles; they will run and not grow weary, they will walk and not faint."

Your present conditions in life right now can determine many things. They can establish what your budget is, where you will eat dinner, the type of car that you drive or the clothes that you wear. But one thing that they cannot have power over is how big you dream or what your future may have in store.

You must dream, and dream with an attitude! Dream real big, and don't let anyone or anything discourage you from what you are aspiring to achieve. When individuals lose their capacity to dream, they are literally giving up on their future.

As you dream, your faith is made stronger. Your hope rises and your praise begins to flow more freely. When you stop dreaming, you will stop praising. When you stop praising, you stop releasing the substance that produces your pearls. When you aren't making pearls, you are one irritated human being. Dream every single day.

2. Drag Yourself to the Place of Outpouring

Matthew 26:40-41 "Then He returned to His disciples and found them sleeping, 'Could you men not keep watch with Me for one hour?' He asked Peter. 'Watch and pray so that you will not fall into temptation. The spirit is willing, but the body is weak.'"

Our spirits are eager for renewal, but our bodies would rather lie down. In order to live a lifestyle of pearl manufacturing, you must drag yourself to the place of outpouring and force yourself to do it even when you would rather do something else.

Jesus' own disciples whom He hand picked fell into the trap of sleeping when they should have been shadowing their Master and ministering to Him.

If an oyster releases his substance, and only does it for a few short months, then stops because he feels like he needs a break; he will not complete the pearl making process.

When we, as Christians, don't constantly push ourselves to be renewed through our praise and worship, we short stop the process, and settle for less than what God has planned for us.

A few years ago, I decided that I needed to lose weight. I joined a gym, and worked out about five days a week. I counted my calories and ate only low fat foods keeping this up for about a year. I worked out when I didn't want to. I didn't overeat. The inches and unwanted pounds began to melt away. However, I became weary in doing well. I started slacking in my exercise regimen. I began eating more desserts and increasing my calorie intake. The effects were exactly opposite of what I had been working so hard to accomplish.

This undisciplined lifestyle slowly crept up on me, and I allowed it to each day. Before I knew it, I was back to my old habits. Everyone starts out on the right track. They are focused and ready for any challenge that they may encounter. Nevertheless, they begin to slack and before it is even realized, they are sleeping just like Jesus' disciples.

Enjoying the Benefits of Supernatural Bethesda

We have an over abundance of people who are miserable, irritated, unhappy, depressed, and just plain wretched. There is absolutely no reason for this to be happening in the lives of God's redeemed people. God has chosen us to be His own special people.

Can you imagine how foolish it would have been if this invalid in John 5 would have looked up to see the Supernatural Bethesda and he would not have taken advantage of this opportunity? It would have been insanely crazy. He waited his entire life for his desire of a miracle to be manifested, and this was his opportunity. He had one chance, on this day, to acquire the very thing that would change his life forever.

God's desire is that you refuse to hangout beside the Bethesda waters of what this world can provide for you. Your Supernatural Bethesda is ready to move in and do for you what no one else is capable of. Don't be discouraged if your triumph is slow in coming. Instead, just continue to give God your advanced praise, thus releasing your substance, and before you even realize it, you will be one more equipped and readied individual as you move on into your destiny.

❧16❧

PAM WAUGH

The Refining Fire of a Loving God

S ometimes we don't know we are being refined by the fire. We think we are being punished and don't deserve the good things God has for us. At least that was me. I was being refined, but felt I deserved every bad thing I got and that God was judging me instead of refining me. What I didn't realize at the time was that God was actually trying to get my attention.

I had lived all my life trying to please God; trying to make Him happy and living by His rules. I had raised my children by the rules and they loved God with all their heart, so what was wrong with me? How could I actually raise two wonderful girls who loved God, and all the while miss it? You see, in my eyes God was based on judgment and works, not on love and His amazingly undeniable, unconditional love for me. I had to earn His love. I had to deserve it!

I'm thankful for God and His pursuit for me. I'm thankful for a God who never gave up on me even though I had a ton of bitterness and anger in my heart. I had lived a life trying to live up to everyone's standards; including God's, and all I felt like at the end of it all was one big failure. I was never going to be that perfect person. I was never going to be good enough. My childhood was full of hurt, disappointment, and pain and I was still living there. I was still that wounded girl and I was still trying to make everyone happy with me because I was just supposed to. I was taught to.

One day I just had enough. My world came tumbling down. I couldn't be perfect anymore. I couldn't live with the tormenting thoughts of what an awful, terrible person I was and I plummeted. I went down. I hit a wall of depression and hopelessness that I thought I could never come out of. I was desperate and I had tried everything, so I thought, and I just couldn't do life anymore. I was so full of hurt, disappointment, pain and suffering that I decided it just wasn't worth living anymore. This was when the fire began. It started to burn away the old person, and refine a newly created woman in God.

When we grow up, some of us have terrible, awful things come into our lives that we don't plan. At eight years old my life changed forever because of a man whom I trusted very much. He molested me and from that day on I took on the shame, guilt and dirtiness that he put on me. Satan had taken an opportunity in my life to tell me that I should be ashamed, guilty, and should feel dirty. As a child I accepted this and decided it was mine to carry. The problem was that when this happened, it never went away. When I became an adult, I still carried it around because I didn't know what to do with it. I didn't know where to put it down. Then I had other times of severe trauma in my life and I ended up carrying those things around with me also. I carried them around as a child and as an adult, until one day the load got so heavy that I collapsed. That was when the fire started.

I realized then that the only hope I had left was God. If God didn't work, it was over, it was done with! I decided then to allow God to take me through the fire; to walk me through the fire while refining me into what He had created me to be in the first place. All these people had made me someone else other than what God had created, and I needed God to burn away all the awful things that people had put on me. When He got done burning up all the mess in my life I wanted Him to leave only what He had created, which as the Bible says is "fearfully and wonderfully made!" (Psalms 139:13) God was going to refine me from the inside out and He did!

I can remember how He taught me. I realized that all good things come from God. I realized that He's not out to punish me at every turn. I realized that He loves me with a love that no one else has for me and that He's a very personal God who reaches all of us in a different way. You see, God knew I needed a daddy that loved me because I had never felt that before. The loving arms of a father who loved me just as I was and a father that I could just crawl up into His arms and he would hold me and make me feel safe! Because instead, I had unsafe things happen to me all of my life, I couldn't even comprehend feeling safe. I could comprehend being depressed, full of anxiety, and panic—but to feel *safe*? That was such a foreign word to me. I even felt unsafe praying because I was always waiting to be punished by God.

Here's the really cool thing about God. He knew all that! I mean, He really knew me and my heart and it didn't bother Him. He just kept reaching out to me more and more and making me feel safer and safer with Him.

In the process of healing He started to teach me to go to Him. I would go to a safe place in my room and I would go to a time in my life when I felt really unsafe and I would tell Him how I felt, like when I was molested. I remember going to Him that day and telling Him how dirty I felt and how I felt so ashamed. This was very hard for me to do. I had never cried before and I had never told anyone the deep dark secret. I was really stepping out into the fire on this one, and I knew I was going to need His hand to be able to stand the heat. I had never faced this fire before and I was scared. I had never trusted God either and I had to step out on faith into the fire. I knew this was the moment of no return. I had to go through the fire. I needed this stuff to be burned off of me if I was going to become who God wanted me to be.

In John 10:10 (KJV) Jesus says "The thief cometh not, but for to steal, and to kill and to destroy, I have come that they might have life and that they might have it more abundantly!" I had decided I was tired of being destroyed, killed, and stolen from and I was going to take my authority back and walk through the fire to get to the other side of abundance in Jesus Christ!

You see, I had to decide. Jesus would help me, but it was my decision. I was tired of being a victim, of being the person God did not create. I was going to claim my identity in Jesus Christ back and I wasn't going to take no for an answer. Something inside me began to well up in my spirit and I knew that God was for me. He was starting to prove to me that He was there for me because I was stepping out for the first time in my life and not accepting all the hurt, pain, and disappoint that Satan had put in my life. I was taking authority with Jesus by my side! He was holding on to my hand as I walked through the fire.

> *I was going to claim my identity in Jesus Christ back and I wasn't going to take no for an answer.*

As I started taking things, all things, even the little things to Him and cried out to Him, He began to heal me. Here's the thing, I used to pray to Him to just fix everything, but I didn't cry out to Him. I didn't give Him my whole heart, I just wanted Him to be my personal genie and fix everything, and do no work. I wanted to live in denial and do nothing. Once I realized that if I went to Him with all of my heart, it made me get real and honest with Him and things started to change. I would cry out to Him but then I would also listen and He would tell me wonderful things! He would always tell me the opposite of all the negatives and He would remind me that I was His beautiful, wonderful, special little girl! I would cry as He would just love on me and it would heal my heart, because for the first time, I knew I was loved.

Loved by God Almighty, the Ancient of Days, and a God that big loved little old me! It was incredible. All the hurt started to burn off as I took it to God, and He took it from me. Everything there was good and it gave me peace and healing. He helped me forgive the people who did terrible things to me. I didn't carry around all the hurt and pain anymore and joy was in my life for the first time ever!

The following verse helped me make it through when things got rough and I didn't know if I could make it. It reassured me that if I kept crying out to God He would be faithful and heal me; and He did! Jeremiah 29:11-14a (NIV) "'For I know the plans I have for you,' declares the Lord, 'plans to prosper you and not to harm you, plans to give you hope and a future. Then you will call upon me and come and pray to me, and I will listen to you. You will seek me and find me when you seek me with all your heart. I will be found by you,' declares the Lord, 'and will bring you back from captivity.'"

I hung onto God having good plans for me and that He wanted to prosper me and not to harm me. So I knew if I went into the fire, He would be there to get me through it and it would prosper me to become the woman of God He wanted out of the fire. I also knew that if I went to Him, prayed to Him, and sought Him with all my heart, and the key word was *all*, then He would hear me. That meant the good, the bad, and the ugly. And you know what? He did! He found me and I found Him. It is incredible when you find God. It is incredible when your life is free of past hurt and pain.

People now ask me "how did you get so happy?" They ask me "how can I get what you have?" And then I tell them. Now people are being set free because I am helping them get refined by the fire and teaching them to allow God to burn up their bitterness, anger, and resentment—the hurt and pain they've carried with them all of their lives. They are experiencing a God who loves them and cares about them also!

Praise God for what He has done, for the fire has refined me into a powerful and free woman of God! I no longer live in depression, anxiety and fear, but in the arms of a loving God!

∞17∞

DONNA DYSON

Anointed to Suffer

In retrospect, I can vividly recall being extremely excited about the hand of God upon my life. I used to enjoy the occasional accolades from people after praying, preaching or ministering—hearing people comment about the evidence of the anointing that rests upon me.

It wasn't until November of 2000, when a sudden relational change had taken place in my life, that I realized that as much as I loved the blessings and favor of God, they come with a spiritual level which can not be escaped, if I planned on staying in the race. While talking to the first lady of our church that night in November, I remember sharing the hurt I was experiencing at that time over a relationship gone bad. I recall her sharing a lot with me that night, but what stuck out more than anything was three words. Those words were "Anointed to Suffer."

Yes, it's true many people are anointed to suffer, but fail to walk in this area of anointing. We have no problem with praying, preaching, ministering, and teaching, but when God allows suffering to come into our lives and we are faced with seasons upon seasons of "going through" circumstances, life changes, and challenges, the last thing we want to own up to is an *anointing to suffer*.

Wouldn't life be easy if all we had to do was wake up and face a day that was filled with sunshine? I know for me it is a struggle sometimes to wake up and face the "whatever" God allows. I often ask God, "When will I have seasons of nothing but favor, blessings, and miracles and by pass the adversities, trials, tribulations, and sufferings?"

God is so awesome, not only does He afford us the opportunity to experience great seasons filled with open doors, prosperity and blessings;

God also keeps us balanced by allowing us to face many trials and tribulations. Jesus reminds us that in this world we will have tribulations, but be of good cheer. This is difficult.

Though I bless God that I am in good health, and typically failing health is not the area in which God allows suffering to come into my life, I experience intense storms, which often forget to end.

The end of 2001, my husband and I found out that we were going to have a baby. The pregnancy itself was difficult, emotionally and physically. My husband was never home during the pregnancy and was sent overseas most of the time. In addition, I started having pre-term labor and became very familiar with the hospital staff.

Finally, the moment we waited for, prayed for, and hoped for had arrived. I gave birth to a beautiful baby boy. He was perfect to me. He spent his first few days in NICU, but even with that I trusted God. My suffering began when the doctor looked at me and said we are almost 100% sure that your son has Down syndrome. Around everyone I was the perfect Christian. I said what I was supposed to say as a minister; "I will handle whatever God has allowed," but when everyone left, my suffering became evident.

> *Around everyone I was the perfect Christian.*

I spent countless hours alone with this beautiful child, and with God, not knowing what I was supposed to do. I became angry with God, with my husband and with people. I didn't understand why God would give me a child with special needs. After all, when I said, "God any way you bless me I'll be satisfied" that was not what I had in mind. I did not realize until three months later that God trusted me so that He allowed me to share in the fellowship of His suffering.

My recent experience with God as an equalizer made me realize that our lives were not meant to be free from the stressors of this world. Our very stressors and trials are ordained for a divine purpose. I remember during this period that I needed answers and I felt as if God had shut me out completely. I remember sitting on my sofa after my son's first group of providers came out to assess him, crying out to God, "Why me, what did I do?"

God spoke to me through His Word. He took me to John 9:1-3 when Jesus and His disciples passed by a man who was blind from birth. His disciples raised the question, "Rabbi, who sinned, this man or his parents, that he was born blind?" What blew my mind and helped me was Jesus' response. Jesus said, "It was not that this man sinned, or his parents, but that the works of God might be displayed in him." In other words, my suffering was not because of something that I did wrong, nor anything that my son had done, but it was so God would get the glory out of my son's life.

Though many of us shout about the blessings from God, the favor of God, the opened doors, the financial outpouring, the higher levels, and the heavier anointing, we fail to receive the full power from embracing our trials. Who would dare celebrate because they are anointed to suffer? It's amazing, we know the outcome of suffering with Christ, we understand that trials come to make us stronger, but we continue to try and rush through the very obstacles that are allowed and put in our space to redirect our attention to our first love.

I would dare to even say that the attention and credit that we give to the enemy for trials has been inappropriately shifted to a spirit that can only operate in the lives of God's people, when given permission. One of the best things that God could have done in my relationship with Him and in my ministry to Him and for Him, was to trust me to experience another attribute of His; longsuffering.

Suffering is not only physical, but also physiological, emotional, spiritual, and mentally; and though some people are actually chosen to suffer, and have been anointed to do so, we all have to face some levels of suffering, even if only at a minimal level. Isaiah 48:10 reads, "I have refined you, but not as silver, I have tested you in the furnace of affliction."

Okay, God is speaking and has shared with us that His test comes through the furnace of affliction. In other words, it is through the moments when we feel like we are about to explode if one more thing comes in our life and our backs are against the wall that God is testing us. It is on those days when we lay down to rest and wake up in pain that God is testing how much we are willing to trust Him and allow Him to be for us the strength we need.

I realized that even the level of suffering and adversity that comes into my life is uniquely designed for me; which tells me that God realizes which child can handle a weight increase. Sometimes God will keep us on 5 lb dumbbells until we demonstrate that He can trust us to carry heavier weight. God showed me so much of myself through all of this; mainly the obvious—that process is not enjoyable.

I also found that God allows the trials and tests to remind us of who He is. In October of 2006, I believe I faced what may have been my absolute darkest moment. My grandmother, who was to me my *Barnabas* who encouraged my heart every single day, went home to be with the Lord. After returning from burying her that night, my marriage of six years died as well.

I did not know what in the world was going on, and I was too numb to react, respond, or run. I was completely numb. I felt as if my entire foundation had been removed from me. I wanted to grieve my granny but was not able to just get a good cry out because I had to face the fear of becoming a single parent again; and now figure out once again how I was going to raise not only a teenager, but my wonderful toddler who so many people had already ruled out.

God is showing me that He is everything I need. He has encouraged my heart through people close to me, but more importantly when they were no where to be found, He poured into me the Word I needed.

I received the constant reminder that God is God, and regardless of what we go through, He is still God. He indeed is the author and finisher of our faith. He alone knows our rising up and our lying down—more than what we know about ourselves. God knows what we can handle, more than what we know. God knows how much heat to allow in our lives to keep us drawing closer to Him and how much heat to allow in our space, forcing us to regain our focus. God allows this for His name's sake. In other words, regardless of the test, the trials, or the opposition, our ultimate response should be to give God glory. "In all things give thanks, for this is the will of God concerning you."

God not only wants to know if we trust Him to do His *God stuff*-but if He can trust us in the fire; or if we will walk away from our convictions. Are we going to go through the fire with God or jump out of the fire and take another path? As difficult as trials are, they really do make us stronger. How will you and I be able to testify to the fact of God being a deliverer if we are never in a hard place which requires a rescue effort? James says, "count it all joy"—be joyous because the fruit of our trial produces endurance, maturity, and completeness. There should always be evidence of a trial. There should always be evidence of a storm, of opposition, and of a fire. The evidence is good fruit.

I have discovered on my journey that not only am I anointed to suffer, but I also have been chosen to be a conduit of His Glory, even while I suffer. God wants us close to Him. In realizing now that suffering cannot be escaped, I pray that God will give me peace for any level of pain that is a part of my plight in life. I realize now that every trial, every test, every affliction, every adversity, every storm, has been strategic in fulfilling the plan that God has for my life.

Dear sister, know that every test and every trial is designed to draw us closer to the Redeemer. He is the only one who can settle our spirit in a fiery furnace and bring us out without smelling like smoke while endowing us with more power. Don't think it strange, as Peter says, of the fiery ordeal and the darts that test us but look at it as an opportunity to suffer with Christ.

Sister, as difficult as it is, embrace the trial. Trials don't last always. There is always a verdict in the end. The jury eventually comes in, but even when the jury can't decide on your fate, God has already determined the path that you will take. God knows how we will respond. Jesus has already paid the price and has thrown Himself in front. Jesus wants to know if we are willing to suffer with Him as He has laid down His life and suffered for us. I am so very thankful that God loves you and me so much that He allows us to suffer with Him, so that we will also reign with Him.

"For I reckon, the sufferings of this present time are not worthy to be compared to the Glory which shall be revealed" (Romans 8:18).

❧18❧

Sabrina Dubyak

The Knock That Changed Everything

It was a beautiful Saturday in February-unseasonably warm and bright. The day had started out perfectly, just the way you would want a day to begin, especially if it were going to be the last; or rather the last you would spend with the one person who knew you better than anyone else.

The person, who knew how to finish your sentences, knew when to let you vent and when to reel you back in; the person who knew how to comfort you with just a touch or simply their presence in the room; one who could calm your fears and dry your tears even if they were a thousand miles away; the person who knew your strengths and faults and loved you unconditionally in spite of it all.

For me, this person was my husband—my Michael.

1 Corinthians 13:13 reads, "And now abide faith, hope and love these three; but the greatest of these is love."

No, he was not perfect, but then neither was I—we were perfectly each others. He was my prince, my night in shinning armor, my hero, best friend and lover.

On this day, the third day of February, 2001, my life as I had known it would cease to exist and I would forever be changed. We kissed each other goodbye and with his golf clubs strapped on his back like a book bag, he hopped on his Harley and off to the golf course he went; his second love next to me.

I know right now you're visualizing a man on a motorcycle with a huge golf bag on his back and thinking, "That sounds crazy!" Having done it many times, he was quite the professional.

After a Saturday of working out and running errands, I returned home in the evening around 6:00 pm. It had just turned dark and to my surprise, Michael was not back yet. The temperature had dropped a little with the evening setting in, so I thought he would have beaten me back home.

I recall saying to myself in my head, *I hope he has his wallet with him so that if anything has happened someone would know how to get in touch with me.*

Being an avid motorcycle enthusiast and a rider myself these are things you do think about. I have heard parents say they have had these type feelings when they felt that one of their children may be hurt or sick and if you have ever had this feeling and been right, you know what I mean.

It was a strange feeling, I can't say that I knew something had happened; it was just a thought that quickly went through my mind and a strange sensation.

As I entered the house, grocery bags in tow, I sat them down and went straight to the bedroom to see if he had left his wallet, watch, something. He always made a habit of putting his wedding ring on my thumb when he played golf and this day was no different.

I had his ring on my finger.

I again said to myself, "I hope someone will call me if anything has happened," never for a moment thinking that a day that started out so wonderful, would end taking part of what felt like my soul with it.

I headed to the kitchen to prepare dinner; as long as I live I will never forget that meal. Shortly after I began preparing to cook there was a brief and subtle knock at the door. It so happened that this door opened right into the sunroom adjacent to our kitchen.

Knock, knock, knowing it just had to be Michael I yelled out "come in honey" and again came the knock, knock..."I said come in"...before I could even finish what I was saying the door slowly opened and much to my shock there was man in a law enforcement uniform walking into my home.

Little did I know in the fleeting seconds that passed before he spoke, that this would be the knock that forever changed my life. His words would replay over and over in my thoughts for the remainder of my life.

I had a half smile on my face as I truly thought my husband was playing a joke on me and would be walking in the door right behind this officer. In the moments that followed it seemed like time stood still, his words hung in the air as he asked my name and delivered the news that there had been an accident—and my husband did not make it.

As I walked backwards away from the officer in a stunned and bewildered state, I still truly believed that my husband was going to walk in with that big ear to ear grin on his face and say, "I got you!"

Everything went from real time to slow motion; everything around me stopped. You know you hear people talk about being in shock and you never really quite get it until you've been there. You lose all sense of time and reality, and you believe nothing that's being said to you. You hear it but it makes no sense, you feel as though you've been catapulted into some type of alternate universe where you are free falling into the abyss.

Unfortunately, this feeling of complete and utter despair as if the world has continued moving and left you behind will increase, and then come and go; but more subtly for an undetermined amount of time.

Each person is different when it comes to the grieving process, each of us reaches our destination at a different pace. Grief is something that should never be rushed by others around the person suffering or by the person their self—feeling obligated to be strong.

> *In the grieving process there is very little energy to cultivate a stoic persona...*

In the grieving process there is very little energy to cultivate a stoic persona; and there shouldn't be the need for a person, especially a believer, to feel they are required to do so.

The unfortunate end to the events that took place on Saturday February 3rd, 2001 would be that my wonderful husband Michael had left the golf course with two of his buddies and had been killed approximately five miles from our home, hit by a car on a very small country back road going barely 15mph on his motorcycle.

It is in the times of our greatest despair that we are given the opportunity to grow—when all that we know to be real and solid and true are shaken or taken away. My world was shaken and shattered, my only comfort in the first moments of realization after the shock began to subside was that Michael had accepted Christ and I knew where he was. I knew when he took his last breath here on earth that his next vision was spectacular.

At that moment my faith in God's word was all I had to hold onto in those seconds and minutes. I had no time to question or be angry; but that time would come. We know God's promises to be true and real and we fight against being angry. Yet it is that anger, that fight, that questioning, that will at the end of it all take us right back to the one who knows us better than we know ourselves.

You see, the first knock that ever changed my life was the one I felt in my heart when the Lord brought me to conviction and lead me to acknowledgement and faith in Him; that forever changed my world.

From the age of 14 when I accepted Christ until February 2001, I had never questioned or challenged God's direction in my life or the obstacles He had put before me to overcome. I had always felt that everything I had gone through was for a reason and every event had always strengthened me for the next. I had suffered losses and much hardship in my young life prior to the ones I found myself drowning under now. I had also seen God's love, protection, and His many blessings through so many accomplishments He had helped me achieve.

Through all those events, good, bad and other, never had I been so defiantly angry with God. However, that would be changed by the loss of my Michael; this was the greatest challenge of them all.

You see, as Christians, anger and questioning is something that is very rarely talked about. We don't want to be seen as weak in our faith, we are told "Everything happens for a reason...you can't question God's will...all things work together for the good of those who believe and have faith...God will not put more on you than you can bare."

A very important person in my life made a statement to me during the course of my grief and anger, it was several months after my husband's death and I was telling him how I felt my anger had put such a wedge between me and the Lord. I felt like I had been so angry at the Lord and had questioned His authority and cried out in so much defiance, that the Lord just might not have me back; and my friend who is also my pastor, Dr. Johnny Hunt, said these words to me, "Sabrina, I know you and the Lord knows you, do you think He was surprised when you were angry over the loss of Michael? God knew how you would respond, before you responded." And then he made a statement I will never forget, he said "Sabrina, God can handle your tough talk."

I think God knew it had to come from someone whom I respected and admired more than anyone else. The God that created me and that knows me better than I know myself was expecting me to be angry and to question and to cry out in defiance! God knew, just as those around me knew, what a great relationship Michael and I had. Everyone understood that I would not get past this easily.

I'm not sure who gets the credit for a statement that I have heard quoted many times but it is this, "pain is inevitable but suffering is a choice."

86

Though I was and always will be heartbroken over the loss of my husband, I did reach a point in my own time, when I was able to say to God, "Even though I don't understand why my husband was taken from me and even with the many questions I still want answered, I am going to let it go for now." I asked Him if He would reveal to me in heaven what I could not get answered here on earth. I knew it was time for me to get back to my God; He was waiting with open arms.

I also asked God to help me use what I was going through and the growth that I was experiencing, of being challenged by adversity, to help other people understand that they are not bad Christians if they get angry, question, or even doubt. God may expect that you will be angry, but anger is not a place you can stay. As a believer, anger is not a place that you would want to stay. You have to go through each season of healing to reach the level of closeness to the Lord that will allow you to thrive in your growth.

I never really connected with all the scriptures about valleys and the mountains and how God will allow you to see what you learned in the sadness or lowness of the valley when you reach the next mountain top.

1 Peter 1:7- "These trials have come so that your faith may be proved genuine."

Now I understand completely, valleys will happen to all of us but here is the encouraging part, they are temporary. My valley may not be like any you have experienced but we all have our own valleys that reflect our own walk and it's all a part of God's path for each of us.

We have to remember what God wants most of all is for us to be more dependent and more in love with Him. I often tell people that the only real good that came out of the loss I suffered was that I have a much deeper and closer walk with the Lord; one I would not have had without, at some point, questioning what it all meant.

Had I never been so low and in such a deep, dark and lonely valley, and had I never been so extremely challenged in my faith, I would not have such a deep one on one relationship with my Father God. Only the one true God could bring so much depth and growth out of such a life altering devastation.

Just as the knock at my door on February 3rd, 2001 forever changed my life, it was because I accepted the Lord Jesus when He knocked on the door of my heart at the age of 14 that He sustained me, loved me, guided and protected me when nothing in this earthly world could.

John 16:33- "Here on earth you will have many trials and sorrows; but cheer up for I have overcome the world." (Living Bible Translation)

Remember, valleys do not last forever, joy does come again.

❧19❧

THERESA VOGEL

Giving Your Gifts-Giving Of Yourself

My favorite time of the year is Christmas. The thing I enjoy the most is buying gifts for others and watching them as they open their gifts. Gifts come in all shapes and sizes—some are expensive and showy, some are reasonable and simple. Occasionally, a gift may be poorly wrapped, but when you take off the packaging, you find it contains a cherished unexpected keepsake. Like gifts, we as children of God have various abilities to offer others.

For a time I wondered what my God-given gift was that would benefit the Church and others. I had already accepted Jesus as my Savior when I was 11 years old. It was in 1968 when I attended Vacation Bible School, and it was during that time I was able to comprehend salvation through Christ. Now that I was a Christian, I wondered *what's next*? As I matured as a believer, I learned that we were to use our gifts and talents to serve others. On the outside, my packaging was not perfect. I was born with significant physical birth defects. How could God use me in this seemingly broken body? I didn't have hands or complete legs like everyone else—mine were different.

It all started with my mom and dad. My dad was an American, in the Army and stationed in Germany; and my mother was from Germany. My dad met and married my mom there. They came back to the United States by ship. While my mom was onboard the ship, she became seasick and the doctor gave her a new medicine to relieve her seasickness. Not knowing that she was pregnant with me, my mom took the medicine and about seven months later, I was born. I was born without hands and without legs below my knees. As I became older, with the help of others, I found ways to compensate. Thus, began my life down *resourcefulness road.*

In the early years of my childhood, I was fitted with arm and leg prosthetics. Although the arm prosthetics were functional, I was not comfortable using them—too artificial, too awkward, and my sense of touch was lacking. During my mid-teens, I decided to stop wearing the prosthetic arms and instead, improvised doing every-day activities with the end of my arms—discovering new ways to do routine tasks.

Learning to live with my disabilities has had its ups and downs. Until I was ten years old, I attended a school for children with disabilities where I was accepted and nurtured. Then it was discovered that I excelled in reading and writing; I was then transferred to a 'mainstream' elementary school. In this new setting the classes were fine, but it was difficult to play games with the other kids. Often I would sit on the sidelines and watch the others play hopscotch and jump rope. At times, I would join in if the games weren't fast ones. Usually, I would sit playing with my Barbie dolls or had my nose in a captivating book. The children generally left me alone; I was mostly spared from the hurtful teasing that is often inflicted on someone who is different.

In addition to my physical disabilities, throughout my youth I was rather shy. I was quite the turtle. It wasn't until the end of high school that I was determined to come out of my shell. The catalyst was when a psychologist told me I was so shy that I'd never be able to interact with the public. His conclusion made me resolute in proving him wrong. I sought out situations, i.e. employment, where I could interact with the public. With the Lord's help

> *Although life has handed me a bunch of lemons, I've managed to make a pretty good pitcher of lemonade.*

and Toastmasters, I was able to deal with my shrinking-violet syndrome.

Although life has handed me a bunch of lemons, I've managed to make a pretty good pitcher of lemonade. Because of the support I received as a child from teachers and family, plus my reliance on the Lord from a young age, my view of life has been generally optimistic. I was a good-natured child at heart so looking at life's situations in a positive way seemed to come naturally. Although I held to this mind-set, there were snags along the way.

In my late teens I struggled with accepting my disabilities. Being a teenager, I was bummed that my social life was at an all-time low. I was asking, "Why me Lord? Why do I have to put up with my disabilities? Why was I born without hands and without legs below my knees?" I searched the Bible for answers. After only a few minutes, I came across 2 Corinthians 12:8-9. This passage stood out as if it were 3-D. It talks about Paul having some sort of thorn in the flesh, maybe some type of disability. He asked God three times to remove it, but God had other plans. He said to Paul, "My grace is all you need. My power works best in weakness."

After reading that, everything fell into place. My focus was off my disabilities, and I began appreciating the gift of God's grace. It was a case of Christ's strength moving through my weakness. Now I take my physical limitations in stride. And so through my weaknesses I have become stronger, because of Jesus Christ in my life.

As years ticked by, people gradually began asking me to share my secrets of maintaining a positive attitude and how it has helped me cope with my disabilities. I felt this was a wonderful opportunity to share my daily walk of faith, in addition to how I handle life's curve-balls. Several years ago, I had attended a church seminar on determining one's spiritual gifts. This led me to the discovery of my spiritual gift of encouragement. These distinctive themes blended well together.

In addition to occasional public speaking, I discovered my talent for creative writing. This too would open up opportunities to exercise my gift of encouragement. In the early 1990's, I taught Sunday school to second and third graders. Instead of teaching a lesson verbatim from the lesson curriculum, I would often create a skit from the lesson to make it more interesting and memorable for the students. This started me down the path to discover my skills in creative writing.

It was not until 2000 that my creative writing talent kicked into first gear. I sensed the Holy Spirit guiding me to expand my writing skills. I started writing inspirational poems, and then songs. After that I began crafting stories. Throughout my early years in school, I was quite the bookworm—I read almost incessantly. Creative writing seemed to come to me rather easily. To validate my talent, I shared my inspirational writing with others and received positive comments. I felt this was another way the Lord wanted me to share my faith. This latent gift blossomed when I was in my early forties.

The Book of Ecclesiastes says there is a time and season for everything. Sometimes our gifts and talents don't appear until later in life and sometimes they become evident earlier. Usually our spiritual gifts develop over a period of time. They become more apparent as circumstances bring them to fruition—ready for God to use them for His glory.

An example that comes to mind is what Corrie ten Boom endured in the Nazi prisons and concentration camp during World War II. She went through the most awful era in history, but God was there with Corrie and got her through that dreadful time. I believe Corrie's spiritual gift was her faith—it was brought to the forefront of her life while she was enduring those horrifying years in the prisons and concentration camp. Because of her faith in the Lord, she was able to share with us those experiences, to let us know God will be with us in all types of trouble.

I have a friend who has a flair for sewing; she makes lovely quilts and frequently gives them to people in need. I know someone else who has a beautiful voice and shares her gift of vocal music. God can use our hands, feet, ears, eyes, mouth, heart and mind for His glory. Whether your talents are great or small, God can use them all.

Some people allege that they don't have any abilities—they claim that God skipped over them when He distributed gifts and talents. This is a misconception. Every person in the body of Christ has God-given abilities. You just need to discover what they are.

When you are not sure where to begin your talent search, start with prayer. Ask the Lord through His Holy Spirit to help you discover your gifts and talents. Study the spiritual gifts that are stated in the Bible; 1 Corinthians 12 is a good place to start. Concentrate on those gifts that appeal to you. It can be a process of elimination. Furthermore, we often recognize our talents and gifts by what we enjoy doing. When you find a talent you enjoy and do well, share it with others and ask for their feedback. Trusted friends and family often provide a safe way to try out a newfound aptitude.

God can use our gifts and talents no matter how insignificant we think they are. God can use us no matter what we look like on the outside. In 1 Peter 4:10 it tells us "Each one should use whatever gift he has received to serve others, faithfully administering God's grace in its various forms." When the members of the body of Christ use their abilities to serve others, they are helping to fulfill the ministry of Jesus Christ. We are His extension in reaching out to the church and beyond. Discovering my abilities and giving to others through them, I can have the feeling of Christmas anytime of the year—you can too! The gifts I give are from my heart and soul.

༻20༺

SAUNI RINEHART

Alone in the Pew

The Bible tells us that we're to "not give up meeting together" as believers (Hebrews 10:25), and I'm privileged to attend a church where I worship with a wonderful group of Christ-followers. But even though I'm surrounded by these brothers and sisters in Christ, I often feel very alone: because, I sit in the pew without my husband.

When Russ and I began dating in 1985, I was as far away from the Lord as I could be. I'd committed my life to the Lord as a six-year-old child, but experiences with sexual abuse had taken me on an often-painful detour. When we first met, I was attracted to Russ' sense of humor and intelligence, and I fell in love with his loyalty and ethics, but in many ways, Russ was the final "fist in the face of God." He had knowledge of God and of Christianity, but he also had some fundamental issues with the faith. Ironically, when he and I were dating, he told me that I would someday return to the faith of my childhood.

Eight years later, he was right. Five years into our marriage, I attended a women's retreat, and the Holy Spirit touched my heart in a way I'd never felt before. That September evening, I recommitted my life to the Lord, beginning a relationship with Jesus that grows ever stronger every day.

The first few years after that decision, I tried to "save" Russ. I preached at him, begged him to come to church, nagged him, gave him books. I would try to talk to him about my recommitted faith and how God had blessed me—how He'd blessed us together. He'd debate intelligently, and when I couldn't support my faith with reason, he'd "push my buttons." Rather than respond with patience and gentleness, I'd snap at him, "Why can't you just believe that what I say is true?"

I'd react in frustration and walk away, and he'd win another round. I was probably worse than someone who'd found the Lord for the first time. I knew what I'd missed through my years of rebellion, and I didn't want Russ to spend another moment without the peace and joy I now felt. So I'd push and prod, gripe and cajole. Nothing worked. In fact, I was probably guilty of pushing him farther away.

Even more, I'm ashamed to say that the Enemy used my frustration against me. There were moments when I'd walk away in despair, and a voice would whisper, "He'll never come to accept Christ, you know." When I'd sit alone in church, it would whisper again, "Wouldn't it be better if you were sitting next to your husband? And if Russ never accepts Christ, wouldn't it be better if you were married to someone else?"

I almost allowed that voice to make me question my marriage, but Jesus is greater than the one who is in this world. Finally, I realized that I couldn't save Russ; that was between him and God. I could only live a life through which Christ could shine. More importantly, I needed to remain committed to my marriage. Paul wrote in 1 Corinthians, that a "woman who has a husband who is not a believer and he is willing to live with her, she must not divorce him. For the unbelieving husband

> *Finally, I realized that I couldn't save Russ; that was between him and God.*

has been sanctified through his wife . . . How do you know, wife, whether you will save your husband?" (7:13-14a, 16a) Now again, I can't save him myself; salvation comes only through the belief in and acceptance of Jesus Christ. However, my actions can influence him to want to know more about a relationship with Jesus Christ.

But I won't kid you; it isn't easy. Anyone who is married to someone who doesn't share her faith knows this well. When you love someone with all your heart and you can't share with him the most important thing, well, it's painful.

Sitting in church Sunday after Sunday . . . all alone. Wanting to be involved in couple's Bible studies . . . but unable to. Seeing a verse that touches your heart . . . and not being able to share it.

It's hard. Really hard. As hard as it is, however, I've learned so much in the years since I recommitted myself to the Lord. It's hard, but I choose to be with Russ. I choose to spend my life with this man whom I love dearly. And I pray every day that the Lord will continue to work in his heart, that he will one day soon know Jesus.

Because when that day comes—and I believe it will—what we have now, the strong marriage and deep love will be even stronger and deeper. My husband supports me even in things that he doesn't agree with, like my speaking ministry and drama ministry at church. If he's that supportive now, I can only imagine how he'll be when he "gets it." If he loves me that much now, I can only imagine how much he'll love me when our marriage is centered on the Lord.

God is faithful. Even when I was the farthest away from him, He had a plan to bring my special husband into my life. And as painful as some of my past has been, I believe that I had to go through what I did so that I could meet and marry Russ. And so that Russ could meet Jesus.

Are you alone in that pew? Does your heart break knowing that the person you love most on this earth doesn't share the most important thing: your faith? Let me share with you what I've learned:

What You *Can't* Do

- **You can't save him, as much as you'd like to**. It truly is between him and God.
- **You can't convince him through nagging or advising or counseling**. If anything, it will alienate him further. Many men don't want to be proven wrong, and your telling him what he should do is only going to turn him off.
- **You can't sway him by slipping books on his nightstand**, no matter how theologically sound those books might be. Believe me, I've read most of the popular books on evangelism and apologetics, and while they've certainly helped me—and may help you—unless your spouse asks for resources, those books will only collect dust.
- **You can't force him to associate with other Christians**. For a long time, I'd ask Russ to join me at church so that he could meet other believers, hoping that, somehow, they'd "rub off" on him.
- **You can't listen to the voice of the Enemy**. Know that Satan would like nothing better than to discourage you, to convince you that your husband will never know Christ. Combat his lies with scriptures, such as the one from 1 Corinthians mentioned above or John 3:16.

However, lest you think that there is nothing you *can* do, read on.

What You *Can* Do

- **You can learn more about your God and your faith**, so that you're prepared to answer any questions that arise. As I've tried to win my husband for the Kingdom, I've studied the Bible. I've read books by wonderful men and women of faith. And my faith has grown stronger and stronger.

- **You can learn to be the person that God has called you to be by understanding your gifts.** When I discovered my gift for encouragement, I began to speak more about how God has worked in my life, and that speaking led to starting my ministry. Although he might not admit it, Russ has watched God's faithfulness through that ministry, and he's even commented once or twice how many 'coincidences'—what I call the hand of God—have occurred.

- **You can serve God and become more and more like Christ.** As I focus on God's plan for my life, I want to be what He wants me to be. I want to live to glorify Him. I find I'm more patient and loving toward Russ—and he sees it. Whether he realizes it or not, my faith has made me a better wife.

- **Most importantly, you can pray persistently and consistently for your spouse's salvation.** I pray for Russ every day—sometimes several times a day. I pray for his health and his work, but I pray diligently for his heart to be softened and to be opened to the truth.

Yes, for now, each Sunday, I go to worship my faithful Father. And, for now, I sit alone in the pew. But I have faith that God loves Russ more than I ever could. I cling to the words in 2 Peter 3:9: "The Lord is not slow in keeping his promise, as some understand slowness. He is patient with you, not wanting anyone to perish, but everyone to come to repentance!" And I pray that someday, I won't sit in that pew alone.

✌21✌

LAKEISHA A. MOORE

A Good, Bad Day

It was supposed to be a good day. After all, I had awoken that morning with a renewed determination to make the best out of what many people term "blue Monday." Joyfully reciting the scriptural mantra "This is the day that the Lord has made," I felt the fusion of purpose and peace combining to safeguard my path, to what I hoped would be a great day in the Lord. As I drove to work, I engaged in worship designed to set the atmosphere for the presence of God that I believed to be sufficient to handle every task and challenge that I might face at work that day.

Excited about the gift of yet another day of life, I anticipated "showers of blessings" to drench my path and unanswered prayers to, finally, open with responses for my life. On my way, I thought about what miracles would unfold on this day. The day seemed too anointed with divine possibilities to be called something as ordinary as "Monday." No, there had to be more to this day than just the start of another 40-hour work week!

Sounds like the framework for a "perfect" day, doesn't it? Unfortunately, before I entered into my office building I literally hit the concrete of the painful reality that it takes just as much work to be optimistic as it does to maintain the perception.

Cue the curtains. Enter stage left: my bad day. As I stepped out of my car with my purse, keys, and BK breakfast meal in hand, I took a big fall courtesy of an oil puddle the size of a small stream that I mistook for a puddle of water in the parking lot. Saving face, I decided to jump to my feet quickly. After all, no one would notice—not even that crowd of people also making their way toward the employee entrance where I had failed miserably at oil skiing. As I examined myself for broken bones, sprained ankles, or more importantly, the tragedy of a ruined breakfast sandwich, I noticed that none of the above had resulted from the fall, just a few bumps and bruises, a big heap of embarrassment, and a ruined pair of light blue scrub pants covered in black oil.

I toddled along toward the entrance; this time with slow, cautious strides to prevent further humiliation. A gentleman, kind enough to open the door for me, upon seeing my pants stained in oil commented, "Wow, you must have really taken a dive out there! What a way to start a day!" I gave a sideways smirk which translated, "Gee, thanks for the word of encouragement! I feel so much better! Never mind that I have to walk around all day looking like I've been rolling around in a dumpster!" Officially, it was a very bad day!

Was this really the day that the Lord had made for me? Did God really intend for my day to exist under the gloom of a clumsy misstep? Where was the balm of optimism to soothe and rejuvenate my spirit? As I inquired of the Lord these things, I could not help but to brace myself for worse things to come during my work day. Besides, I would have to replay the incident over and over again as my coworkers questioned my 'new' fashion trend and I was not in the mood to narrate the drama.

> **Was this really the day that the Lord had made for me?**

Later that night, God began to minister to my heart as I recalled the dreadful events of my day. He challenged me to mirror my day with the worst day in all of human history: the crucifixion of Jesus Christ. God provoked me to weigh the severity of my bruises to the unmerited torture of every inch of Jesus' flesh. Instantly, I realized the needless attention I had given to such a trivial event in parallel to the brutal massacre demonstrated at the cross. Indeed, Jesus had the worst day, but not without a greater purpose at work behind the scenes— the power of His resurrection renouncing the death penalty of sin and reconciling the relationship of God and mankind.

So, how did Jesus handle His rough day? The Gospel of Mark records Jesus "flipping the script" on defeated days forever: "Don't be alarmed," He said. "You are looking for Jesus the Nazarene, who was crucified. He has risen! He is not here. See the place where they laid him" (Mark 16:6 NIV).

First, Jesus realized that the wisest way to handle a bad day was not to wallow in self-pity or constantly complain, but to exit death's grave and enter into the world of good day victories. We too must align our daily perspective with the understanding that we have already overcome any obstacle, impossibility, and (oil slick!) that seeks to curse our days with darkness and disappointment. We have overcoming power through Christ's resurrection that no amount of hell in the course of our days can dilute or destroy.

Secondly, Jesus left behind everything that reminded Him of His bad day. When the disciples examined the empty tomb of Jesus, they noticed that the garments that were used to wrap His body still remained in the place where He was laid. These garments had no use for the resurrected Jesus. Likewise, we must abandon useless attitudes, thoughts, words, and actions that reflect the "old nature" of sin which has been crucified with Christ. Rather, we must take only what pertains to the "new man" of the resurrection that is joy, peace, righteousness, and unwavering faith. As Jesus declared after His resurrection, "All power is given unto me in heaven and in earth." This power restores our belief in the God who purposely crafts our days; each one different from the next with a "built-in" feature that's able to withstand the turbulence of stormy days.

Recently, my Pastor challenged the congregation in his Resurrection Day sermon to walk everyday in the resurrection of Jesus Christ; not just on Easter Sunday. What did he mean? We are commissioned by God to reflect the evidence that the empty tomb of Christ opens the dimension of limitless possibilities for our lives. Because He lives, we can live on the pulse of divine purpose, fulfill our destiny, and look forward to the good days to come—oil soaked pants optional!

❧22❧

NANCY KAY GRACE

Resting in the Refuge

The phone call disturbed my quiet afternoon and changed my life. "I have some bad news and some good news." The doctor's calm voice sounded serious. He had my attention. I sat down at the kitchen table and picked up a pen to write down what he would tell me.

"The bad news is that it is cancer, but the good news is that we got it all and it's very treatable."

He continued explaining the diagnosis to me, but my mind had frozen on his first statement. *Cancer?* I choked back tears and scribbled his medical words on a notepad. *Tongue cancer?* Being a woman, I had considered the possibility of other kinds of cancer, but never this.

Preoperatively, the doctor thought the nagging sore on my tongue was an ulcer and almost did not send it in for a biopsy. After all, I did not fit the profile for tongue cancer. First, he chose non-invasive treatment. After there was no improvement, he surgically removed the sore.

I struggled to form the words to talk with the doctor, with the stitches and swelling in my tongue. After hanging up the phone, I needed a safe place for God to restore me—again.

This was another in a series of crisis events for me. The past year had been difficult. My father passed away the morning after a successful cancer surgery, and then several months later my mother faced serious health issues. Now I suddenly found myself in this unexpected health situation. This all left me spiritually and emotionally empty; and physically drained.

Pulling myself together, I spent intense time seeking God that night. Tears and questions washed over me as I prayed. In the midst of crying out to God, the passage Philippians 4:6-7 came to mind:

"Do not be anxious about anything, but in everything, by prayer and petition, with thanksgiving, present your requests to God. And the peace of God, which transcends all understanding, will guard your hearts and your minds in Christ Jesus."

A gentle but powerful exchange occurred in my heart as I released my anxiety through prayer. The Lord accepted my "what if" questions and replaced them with the precious gift of the deep assurance of His presence. I experienced the "peace that passes understanding" in a way I had never known. I found an inner sanctuary that became a refuge in God.

The Psalms had brought me hope many times during this season of crisis. David often refers to God as being a refuge or dwelling place. I learned several principles from Psalm 84.

"How lovely is your dwelling place, O Lord Almighty! My soul yearns, even faints, for the courts of the Lord; my heart and my flesh cry out for the living God. Blessed are those whose strength is in you, who have set their hearts on pilgrimage. As they pass through the valley of Baca, they make it a place of springs…they go from strength to strength…" (Psalm 84: 1, 2, 5-7)

Seeking a Refuge

How often my heart cried out for the presence of God during those difficult times! The first verses of Psalm 84 speak of seeking a *dwelling place*, or *refuge*, near the Lord. With each incident, the Lord calmed my heart with His promises of peace and security. Quiet time with the Lord became even more important; this was my refuge for daily communion with God. Even in my confusion and despair, the God of the universe did not remain far off, but He gave me His peace and assurance in the protected shelter of His love.

Psalm 91:1-2 says "He who dwells in the shelter of the Most High will rest in the shadow of the Almighty. I will say of the Lord, 'He is my refuge and my fortress, my God. In whom I trust.'" Seeking refuge in God became my purpose.

Restoration of the Heart

I knew the replenishment of my emotional and spiritual strength could come only from God. I had little strength of my own. Psalm 84:5-6 describes the *restoration of the heart*. The "Valley of Baca" mentioned in this Psalm actually means a valley of weeping. The promise in these verses is that the place of weeping becomes "a place of springs." There *will* be hope in the difficult places. I had many days in my personal "Valley of Baca," but overcame despair and fear by seeking refuge in the living water of the Word of God. Intentional time spent reading scripture, praying, and journaling brought steady healing to my soul. The desolate valley of my personal struggle for hope became a place for restoration. With the hope from restoration, I gained the perspective that God would use these trials for His good in my life.

The Refining Process of Faith

Psalm 84:7 describes the *refining process of faith*. The Psalmist speaks of going from "strength to strength." The secret is found in the little word *"to."* While we clearly enjoy the mountaintop experiences of life, more time is spent living *in between* the mountaintops, going from strength *to* strength.

God uses the events in our lives to forge our character and to learn to trust His character in new ways. As I passed through the valley of each crisis, I learned more about God's faithful nature and saw how deeply He cared about me. He was re-shaping me with each situation.

I had the assurance I would come out from these struggles stronger in faith and trust in the Lord, like the new butterfly appearing from the chrysalis. Struggle is needed for the butterfly to fly free from its cocoon; as it emerges, its wings rub on the edges of the cocoon. This struggle actually prepares its wings for the next stage of life. It goes from strength as a caterpillar, through struggle, to strength of being a beautiful new creation. Likewise, struggles can refine and transform us to become a new handiwork of God, with greater hope and strength.

> *Struggles can refine and transform us to become a new handiwork of God, with greater hope and strength.*

Focus on Restoration

The promise in I Peter 5:7 puts the concept of going from "strength to strength" in perspective: "And the God of all grace, who called you to his eternal glory in Christ, after you have suffered a little while, will himself restore you and make you strong, firm and steadfast."

The promise of restoration after suffering gives us hope! The pilgrimage of my faith has taken me through dark valleys, but my faith is deeper and my joy stronger from learning to rest in His refuge. The Lord has restored my weary heart once again and I am more steadfast, refined by the fire of His sustaining love.

My tongue healed with minimal speech difficulty, although I gradually had to re-train my tongue to say certain words. The cancer episode occurred at the beginning of my speaking ministry. But rather than abandon what God would have me do, I became more motivated to use my faltering tongue to proclaim God's grace and faithfulness. This could only happen through resting in the refuge.

❧23❧

CONNIE L. VAN BERKEL

Trials of Victory

My sister, Bonnie, and I were born to loving parents, yet that parental love was tempered by our father's addictions. My father and mother were both Christians who were raised in the church, yet our home did not reflect Godly life. I found that Church, a norm for Bible belt kids in Texas, provided a safe haven. It was home. At eight years old, hoping for God's comfort from our home life marred with alcoholism and gambling, I asked for a Bible for Christmas. My faith journey with a Bible gifted by my grandparents began Christmas morning with *In the beginning...*

A succinct way of speaking about our life was that often when our father had difficulties with life, drinking and arguments ensued. I would cling to my Bible and sister, praying God would deliver us from this nightmare. Bonnie and I worked and I do mean *worked* at not upsetting our father and mother. We were good children who followed the rules and never talked back to our parents. Our family loved each other, but not until I was older did I understand why my father had these addictions. As I learned, children of alcoholics face their own demons. Sins of the father carry through to many generations. Only The Lord can alter life's outcome and bring us into victory.

Ever the vivacious Texas girl, I looked to the Lord for "how to live victoriously" in the midst of my home life. Bonnie, however, struggled as a victim in life making weak choices to the point of attempting suicide. Not until I was a teenager on a sleepover did I know what life was like without an alcoholic, gambling parent. The yearning for a different home life pressed hard into my heart.

My teenage years encompassed the usual angst, frustrations with parents, church, dating, college and decisions about life. Vietnam, the sexual revolution, and the anti-authority mindset were in full bloom.

Needless to say, that time in American history proved to be a turning point for many young people, including me. I ensconced myself in the church, the one haven from family and life. At Lafayette United Methodist Church in Lafayette, CA, my spiritual gifts of teaching, administration, evangelism and leadership were born. Over time the Lord grew me into these gifts to bring glory unto Him.

Through a wonderful youth minister, I learned the Lord had a plan for my life. I was thrilled with that good news, but in my life choices I often trekked alone on faith's journey except for God, scripture and prayer. You might say that's powerful, but sometimes I longed for an earthly shoulder and confidant to share and discover victory in the journey and assuage the loneliness. In hindsight I understood how God provided; and through that understanding I recognized the awesome providence of God in the journey.

In my 20's I learned about addictions and why people succumb to the lure of "well-being" through them. I asked God to show me how to love my father and see my father through His eyes because I knew He loved my father. Through a humble spirit, revelations unveiled as to why my father, his brother and sister each embraced addictions to compensate for their childhood and upbringing. The depression and World War II added to their home life problems I'm sure. Their home was not a welcoming place and parent approval was a missing component.

As I grew in understanding God revealed the hurt my father endured. Even as a brilliant and successful man, he couldn't cope with life without those addictions. My mother's coping responses to that situation impacted my life too. I learned to be a people-pleaser, guard against anger situations, never upstage a man, avoid being a woman who thinks and acts on her own. I was frustrated. I inwardly screamed that I was smart, had lofty thoughts, life aspirations and dreams. And, I knew in my heart without a doubt that God held me close. He exposed a life journey different than what my mother and father defined for me.

Life experiences challenged my faith. Hard lessons were learned, but through all I knew the Lord was with me. He would not let go, and for that I am thankful. Not all choices were wise or good, but God forgives those who come before Him seeking forgiveness and accepting His mercy. In those experiences the thought of "would these experiences drive my father to drink and gamble, and how would my mother compensate?" weighed heavy; and "how would I face the unknowns?" I loved them so much. I learned to be a risk taker and step out of my comfort zone. I learned how to turn those traits into glorifying God through His forbearance.

A boat accident at the age of 18 altered my life and face. The left side of my face needed a unique surgical procedure, performed by only one doctor in the world at the time, to create a normal face and save my eye. The procedure is common now, a blessing for many with broken facial bones. The surgery fixed the obvious, but pain and/or numbness in my face and mouth are life-long results. I had been teaching Sunday school for a while when the accident occurred. The children were excited about knowing Jesus and were enthusiastic about being in Sunday school. The accident would be a time I felt Satan's attack to discourage my Sunday school ministry.

From the time I was a young girl my dream was to be a business owner. Yet, in the 50's and 60's and even 70's a woman didn't possess those types of goals. The drama of what to do with my life proved to be unsettled and complicated. My father wanted me to be a stewardess so that placed me in the difficult position of displeasing my father. My college counselor advised me that women could be executive secretaries, but seldom would become CEOs. Perhaps the idea of owning a business could be accomplished, I thought, but I was discouraged. I felt pushed into situations where others decided my life and circumstances.

> *My college counselor advised me that women could be executive secretaries, but seldom would become CEOs.*

I married an unbeliever at age 19 to escape home life, a willful misstep of faith and a direct departure from the Word about being unequally yoked. In the years that followed I understood that my rebellion to live my life my way was a strong factor in deciding to marry. The marriage produced two wonderful daughters, but proved to be difficult. I am still surprised at how easily worldly living becomes the norm.

Married, a homeowner, 22 years old, and pregnant, I decided to explore the business world. I suppose you could call that risk-taking and multi-tasking rolled into one. I began a small sewing concern out of my home. With no experience and no modeling of how to accomplish this, mistakes came. I burned out in a short time. I learned from those mistakes and started again in another industry as self-employed.

After years of worldly living in my marriage, I renewed my love for Jesus Christ and His church. I even began a church group called *Beloved Believers* for married women with unbelieving spouses. Several spouses came to the Lord, including mine, but that did not undo the marriage difficulties. As self-employed during those years I could be an involved mother, volunteer, grow in faith, and learn business processes. I learned that with God anything is possible. However, the 24-year marriage ended in divorce. Although the marriage had been over for ten years before the divorce, it ended with an affair, not a wise choice for me as a Christian. The consequences for that decision are far-reaching, and few understood the life-saving need for the divorce.

My life endured a tragic turn when I became a certified Bethel Bible series teacher. My sister Bonnie died from car accident injuries during Advent of 1984 at 33 years of age. She was unmarried and with no children. The tragedy left us grappling with the loss for years. A harsh time did bring glory to God in that Bonnie, a small woman and donor, gave three young people a fresh start in life because of death. I still yearn to talk with Bonnie and in God's time it will be so. I was proud of my father during the tragic days of the hospital and death events. He didn't drink as far as I know. However, this event colored my parent's lives for the rest of their days, some good and some bad. They endured enough hurts in life, this I knew. I wanted to carry this hurt for them, but God would need to do it. In my observation, it seemed Jesus now had a small role in their lives.

Through the Bethel Bible class the students became leaders in the church, embraced tithing and sought to be leaders of the Word in their homes. How these factors played out over the years I do not know, but at the time the results indicated that my teaching through the Lord's direction inspired a Godly response. Again, I felt Satan's attack through my sister's death. You might be thinking that's an arrogant statement to make, but I assure you that people's intent on serving God undergo attacks.

Today, I am happily remarried. John and I are parents (stepparents) to three married daughters and grandparents to six, with Adeline due to be born soon. We are both ordained elders and Bethel Bible series teachers. My spiritual gifts of teaching, administration and leadership led me to be president of women's groups, write Bible studies and programming, and be a dynamic Bible study leader and program organizer. The Lord has used me to lead many to Christ, a humble and rewarding experience in that God would trust me for such weighted eternal circumstances.

Just four years into remarriage, breast cancer altered my life. Five surgeries and six years of follow up therapy proved to be a challenge unequal in my Christian journey, but I was determined to glorify God through the experience. I suffered significant memory loss that required years of study to regain knowledge...not an easy task while working, two-three hours sleep a night, depression and pain. Through the cancer experience, people watched me: some came to the Lord, some went back to church, some began to pray. I am thankful God was glorified which was my prayer from the first moment I heard the diagnosis.

My 36-year career reflects the realities of being a professional Christian woman in the workplace. Besides self-employment, I've worked for private, public and religious entities. Bringing Christ into my work life and lessons learned has helped pave the way for my daughters to succeed in their workplaces. Along this journey I grew and gained skills; and realized that many Christian women were on the same journey. The seeds were planted by God and nourished into the book *Choose High Road Victories*…

I am thankful for my parents and for learning to live in victory through trials. Victory living is not easy at times, nor did God say it would be. I would not change a moment of my life. Through God I live today victorious and forgiven by His continued molding of me into His child. As imperfect as I am (and still making mistakes), I have seen God turn people-pleasing into pleasing and showing respect for Him, anger situations into proper assertive behavior, upstaging a man into embracing spiritual gifts, and empowered to be the woman He has created me to be.

God granted me a special blessing when I saw my mom for the last time before God took her home. We read the scriptures and prayed together for the first time. I'm blessed by God and His son Jesus, who calls me by name, Connie, child of God.

❧24❧

CHRISTINE KUMBIN

Born for a Cause

Thoughts are like trains— they take you somewhere. When I was nineteen, I was alone at home. I had just graduated from college. I began to think about why God created me. I thought that God had created me for a simple, singular purpose…to raise a 'little girl' up. The more I pondered on this, I developed more thoughts on it. Then my thoughts began to stretch and develop. The Holy Spirit began to teach me and show me that I was created for more than this…for more than I thought of myself, and for more than I thought, have ever thought, or imagined (Eph. 3:20).

Then the Holy Spirit began to unveil to me that God had a bigger reason for creating me. I didn't know at the time, but as I continued to go to church and keep myself focused on God and His kingdom, I began to understand and take little steps in my Christian walk, not knowing exactly where they would lead me. One day, my pastor said to me, "He created you for more than this." Then different thoughts began to run through my mind. *Was I doing anything wrong? Why did my pastor say this to me?* My thought was like a runaway train and at that point I heard a gentle voice say to me "God has a more complicated reason for creating you; not just to raise one little girl but to raise other young women too, to give them meaning for life, to source their potentials, and to develop them to full capacity so that they can develop others in turn. This will give them the abundant life that is only found in Jesus." I thought, *Mmmm! Consequently, to give them hope for the future.*

I began to realize and later on understand that the Holy Spirit was trying to teach me something. He was trying to teach me how I could develop a serious hunger for the things of God; so serious that I would be prepared to die for them. The Holy Spirit then started to teach me how I could create space in my life, and clear every rubble on the way, so I could allow God on the steering wheel to fill me up with the kind of compassion I needed, for the kind of service that the Holy Spirit was pointing me to.

The Purpose of Life is a Life of Purpose

As I sat cross-legged in my sitting room reading one of John Mason's books, something caught my eye: "Purpose does what it must, talent does what it can." My thoughts quickly went back to how Jesus discovered His purpose in life, accomplished it by going to the cross and by dying to save us, then resurrecting after death. *He lived His life in heavenly realms and on earth to fully accomplish His purpose. Jesus lived a life of purpose, and in it taught us how to discover our purpose of life,* I thought.

At this point, I started to focus on Jesus' accomplishments, and this did me a lot of good. I felt it was therapeutic. It felt as if someone had opened my brain to put knowledge in; a bit of knowledge about my master, Jesus, who lived a life of purpose. I began to realize that these thoughts were taking me somewhere into God's purpose.

I had begun to understand that Jesus found the purpose of life having lived the life of purpose. A thought came to me that, *We all must discover our purpose in life and live it. It is this life of purpose all of us, including the 'little girl' (whom I thought that I was created for the singular purpose of raising her) must live.* This little girl's mum is my younger sister who got pregnant in a mission school at the tender age of 15; and had this baby, making her a teenage mum. This scenario became a dilemma for her, her family, her school (a mission school), and the society in which she lived.

To be pregnant in a society such as this was a big problem. It carried with it shame, blame, stigma and sometimes, ostracization. Therefore, our dad, a very strict disciplinarian, a medical man, trained by British missionaries and working at a Mission hospital at the time, refused to share the shame, blame, and stigma that were associated with pregnancy outside of wedlock. He said to my sister in annoyance, "Get out of my house and go to whoever has taught you to behave that way." He dissociated himself from her and sent her away from home. Anybody would think that this was cruel and I thought the same because our dad was very loving. I had never seen him in this mood in all of my life!

Thoughts began to run through me, *How can you treat your own daughter in this manner? Where will my sister go to now? Who would like to help her?* At this point, I began to cry aloud. Our dad didn't think that anything was wrong with his decision. Instead he was angry that his daughter brought shame, blame, and stigma upon the family. Although he loved her, he still wanted to correct her by punishing her and this was the punishment he chose: to send her away from home!

But at a tender age of 15 what did she know about life? Where could she go since she didn't have money and she couldn't fend for herself? She didn't have any experience in pregnancy or childbirth! Worst still, she wasn't in a position to start thinking about her future....she was clouded with so many problems.

I felt so much compassion and pity for her. I therefore ran to my sister's aid and accepted her to stay with me. I was just starting work as a trained teacher, fresh, straight from the oven—oven fresh! On that very morning my sister had her baby at about 6:00 am; a little girl. She also had an English 'O' Level exam paper to write at 8:00 am about 100 miles away! Did I think my sister would make this exam? No. This sounds like a fairy tale but it isn't.

My sister was determined to write this exam because English is a core subject in the West Africa Examination Council {WAEC}. What did this mean? It meant that if you passed all the 'O' Level papers without all the three core papers, you would not gain entrance into a higher school to do your 'A' Levels. After birth, my sister had to travel to her school to write this examination. The most gratifying part of this story is not her safe birth, nor her determination to travel after birth, but the fact that she scored an 'A' grade in the English paper. I looked at her general 'O' Level results in the WAEC Examination, and saw that she had an excellent result. Therefore, I was happy that she would be going to higher school to do her 'A' Levels.

The new baby girl had to stay with me. I found a higher school for her mum, who is my sister, to study her 'A' Levels for a year in order to qualify for a direct entrance into university. My difficulty started then because I didn't have any experience I needed in child care, pregnancy, or any of the sorts. I learned on the job! "Necessity," they say, "is the mother of invention." I therefore, employed the services of one nanny after the other to take care of the baby, all in a bid to get a "good" one; "good" was a relative term because even I didn't know what I was looking for since I had no previous background experience to compare with what I had.

Coupled with this fact was that I was a fresh teacher who just graduated from university and I was in a new environment. I didn't even know anyone in the town yet. That was my first time there. I couldn't call on anyone in the town to help me. I had an inner pain and I can't just describe to you how I felt. I was suddenly forced to grow a baby; forced to mature raw. But God was there for me, He heard my inner cry for help.

Remember that God cares about every detail of your life and will fulfill His plans for you. You need to simply be where He wants you to be and He will do the rest.

Sometimes while I was teaching, the nanny would bring the 'little girl' to the door of the classroom where I taught and the baby would intensify her cry; she would cry loudest when she heard my voice and the students in the class would giggle and giggle. They were having fun but I wasn't; that's not my idea of having fun. At the time, I was just learning how to control my class. I was a novice—a fresh teacher trying to learn the art of classroom teaching.

> *You need to simply be where He wants you to be and He will do the rest.*

Most of the time I felt ashamed of myself because of the baby. Worse still, lots of people around thought it was my child, and that I bore it out of wedlock, and that I was only pretending that I wasn't her mother! It was a difficult and awkward place to be at but we managed. When I say 'we' I am referring to the little girl and I. Soon, the year went by and her mum came back from college to wait for her higher school ('A' Levels) results. Again, her results were excellent, and I was over the moon about this.

You may ask how was my sister's spiritual state now and did she ever make peace with dad and return home? These are important questions that are pertinent to my story. My sister repented to God for her wrong for getting pregnant outside of wedlock and the Lord restored her fully and gave her wholeness. Now she ministers out of that wholeness that can only be found in Jesus. She also made peace with our dad and mum, and she was accepted back home into the family. The little girl was liked by both me, her mum, our parents and the society that rejected both her and her mum.

When the little girl was ready to go to secondary school, I was already the principal of a World Bank Assisted secondary school and I admitted her there. This was a school meant for only the top six students in the common entrance examination from every state of the federation. It was great to have her in this school because she was very clever and grew more in wisdom and stature and the Lord's statutes. I was proud of her at this time and not ashamed. She became a child that brought tremendous blessings to the whole family wherever she went.

My sister went to the university; again she came out in flying colours. She then went to the law school and qualified as a barrister. Now my sister is married to a pastor and has her own law firm. She is doing very well. She has five other children including twin girls, and most importantly, all the members of their family fear the Lord. My sister is now a Pastor and teaches on cable TV/Media.

What about the little girl, you may ask? The little girl graduated as a lawyer, also went to the same law school her mum attended and was called to the bar last year! She currently works at her mother's chambers and is the Youth Pastor at my sister and her husband's church. Too good to be true? No!

This is God in action. He never leaves us nor forsakes us. Part of the reason why He came is to exchange His riches with our poverty; to give us beauty for our ashes. He has really given my sister beauty for her ashes. He has blessed my sister beyond her socks. When a British says that, he means that one has been blessed beyond their measure—the type you couldn't ask, think, or even imagine as mentioned in Ephesians 3:20. When God swings into action, He blesses and blesses and blesses in spite of ourselves. His plans were formed before the foundations of the world. He is the God of the second chance. He did not only restore my sister, but gave her a hope for the future; even the future hope that can only be found in Him.

My joy exploded because both my sister and her daughter's lives were transformed, and I was blessed in the process too. I thought my work was done and I had accomplished what God had asked me to do. Up to that point I thought that God had created me for the singular purpose of raising a little girl; but then thoughts began to run through me again. I started to ask questions on all that had gone before. Also, I started wondering who will do a research in this area to find out more authentic results. These thoughts, led me to do a doctoral research in this area of School-Aged-Mothers; to investigate what the Federal Government of Nigeria was doing for Young Women.

The cause of young women was fast becoming my supreme mission in life. I started investigating and researching about School-Aged-Mothers at Bristol University in England. Once my Research was completed, the results were revealing. I discovered a lot of issues that had to do with customs, traditions, and practices that were in the way of the education and development of young school-aged mothers. This has led to the setting up of my ministry, *Cherished Foundation*, to give these young women a hope for the future.

❧25❦

MARINA WOODS

A Passion for Purpose!

I am a woman on a mission. I realize by the grace of God that I have been created with a purpose and for a purpose. My mission is to glorify God by marketing and promoting books, authors, and resources that affirm biblical values. I am supposed to help people grow spiritually strong and proclaim Jesus Christ as the answer to every human need, to the church and un-churched, through my consulting company and via Good Girl Book Club. This is a web portal and online discussion community designed to inspire and empower young and adult women with articles, author interviews, and fiction and nonfiction books that lead them back to the Word of God.

Stepping out on faith wasn't easy. With so many opportunities available to women today and with the parable of the talents deeply imbedded in my consciousness, there are numerous occasions when I still ask myself, "what if?" What if I become a radio or T.V. show host, what if I sign up for a direct marketing business, what if I become a teacher, etc. Regardless of what path you and I take with the free will God has given us, I have learned that God very rarely drops everything in our laps. Sometimes, even most times, fulfilling our purpose requires obedience, perseverance, total trust and surrender to just get to the next step.

God does not give us the big picture, nor does He expect us to have everything figured out to fulfill our purpose. In a nutshell, what I have learned in the trenches is that the most valuable asset I have on my journey is trust and Hebrews faith in God for *everything*. Childlike faith about sums it up.

113

Refined by Fire: Defining Moments of Phenomenal Women

As long as I can remember I have always (and I do mean always), loved books. I can remember receiving my Walt Disney and Dr. Seuss book selections each month from the children's reading clubs my parents and grandparents signed me up for. To receive two packages with my name on it was a big deal for me as a little kid. *Ahh, that new book smell!* To this day, I still love receiving books in the mail and I can never go to a mall or coffee shop without browsing bookstores. Friends and family ask me, "Don't you *already* have enough books?" Only a person with a mission and passion for book promotion could understand my reasoning.

In retrospect, one could say my purpose was being discovered when my brown package arrived each month when I was a kid, but who knew for sure? In grade school and high school, whenever I would receive my allowance I would head right over to Kroch's and Brentano's bookstore in Evergreen Plaza, near where I lived. I never left the store empty handed either. When I would be placed on restriction, T.V. time was not taken from me—my favorite teen romance novels were!

By the time I was eighteen and moving to a new home, I had collected over 1000 books. I had my very own built-in book case and lounge chair. As I grew older and began to recognize my gift of gab, television and radio began to peak my interest. My mom worked in television at the time, and being surrounded by all those famous people almost pulled me in. When I entered college, God asked me one day, "Why do you really want that?" I realized I wanted to be famous; and to be paid to talk would be wonderful. Yet something else continued to stir in my heart.

I remember clearly two turning points in my adult life. One time, I had taken two mental health days from working at Clear Channel Radio to decompress. I was bored with watching T.V. and began reading an inspirational novel, *Redemption Song*. A few weeks prior, I'd completed *The Prayer of Jabez* and had been praying for an enlarged territory. Two days later, God had answered my prayer for an enlarged territory.

On the third day, a name came to me, then a flashback to a book conference I had attended at South Shore Cultural Center, a weekend or two earlier. I immediately dialed a friend in publishing and asked her to pray for me. God had just birthed something in me and I had no idea what to do! It was way bigger than me (and still is) as I was working in media communications with my sights set on dethroning, Oprah. On that day God gave me two words: Be faithful.

Once I made the mental decision to move forward, over time, I began to notice God-stops. I would meet someone who would lead me to someone else who was an answer to prayer regarding a service I needed to

114

help fulfill my purpose. Next, I would be inspired to submit a press release to a major national publication and days later they would call. Even with these God-stops and more like them along the way showing up right before I would give up, there were still so many times I wanted to give up; that I cried myself to sleep; that I awoke anxious and afraid to face the day. Many times weary, anxious, frustrated, angry, without money, and well, you get the picture. Keep hope alive became my mantra. God did not leave me or forsake me.

I was heading to a meeting with a friend and colleague who had been picked up by Thomas Nelson publishing company. We were on our way to meet with the President of UMI (Urban Ministries), one of the largest African American owned Christian publishing companies. As I looked around the headquarters, I recall the receptionist telling us about UMI's founder who had started his publishing company in the basement of his small home on the Southside of Chicago. He wanted to give up. He even asked God, "why me?" and the response he received was one that God has given me. "Be faithful over little and I will make you ruler over much." Another God-stop!

I have no idea where I would be in life—vocationally or spiritually if I had not sought the face of God to discover and actualize my purpose, or even worse, if I would have abandoned my purpose by not persevering with seemingly immovable obstacles in my path.

As Dr. Jeanne Porter discusses in lesson 2 of *Leading Lessons: Insights on Leadership from Women of the Bible*, God began helping me to network and positioning me at the right place, at the right time, and in front of the right people. As Porter further describes, "the process I was in was working, but it was taking me some time to realize its long term success." Process is an important word to remember when you are being refined by fire. When I read this I vowed, "one day, it will be six months from now and I won't hurt this bad."

That *one day* came, and I didn't hurt as bad!

I am now president of my own company iMarketingPR.com, and I am founder and president of the fastest growing Christian and inspirational book promotions company/community serving and reaching over 125,000 young and adult Christian women worldwide whose lives are being impacted with others coming to know Christ through books that lead them back to the Word of God.

The company has donated hundreds of Christian books and resources to women's shelters and their lives have been changed too. It's only the Holy Spirit at work through me that could do this for people. I truly believe that books and music are conduits of God's grace in our lives.

God kept His promise He made to me the day I walked away from Corporate America with only His words hidden in my heart, truly believing that He had good plans for me, plans for hope and a future and not for harm. There were times I was too broke to pay attention, struggled to make ends meet, angry at God, cried out, "why me!?" and wanted to abandon my faith and the passion for my purpose. I had to take one breath at a time, one step at a time, and one moment at a time- so that I didn't faint and give up.

Fulfilling my purpose didn't happen overnight or over a year, but God kept His word to me moment by moment. I had to and still continue to rely on the Holy Spirit for supernatural strength. I felt fear and did it anyway and I am still doing it anyway. Trust me, all I am to accomplish with the vision I have been given requires going from faith to faith.

> *There were times I was too broke to pay attention, struggled to make ends meet, angry at God, cried out, "why me!?" and wanted to abandon my faith and the passion for my purpose.*

I truly believe that God will do, and is doing the same for you as you persevere with your purpose. Marianne Williamson stated, "Our deepest fear is not that we are inadequate. Our deepest fear is that we are powerful beyond measure. It is our light, not our darkness, that most frightens us. We ask ourselves, who am I to be brilliant, gorgeous, talented, and fabulous. Actually, who are you *not* to be? You are a child of God. Your playing small does not serve the world."

Keep the faith, for this is about putting your life and your purpose on a bigger scale to help other people. May you be blessed beyond measure as you continue to be obedient and persevere with your purpose as a leader. The best is yet to come!

Encouraging Tips for a Passionate Purpose When Faith is All You Have
- Seek God for one or more life Scripture verses to stand on. My four are: Matthew 6:33, Jeremiah 29:11, Mark 11:23-24, Habakkuk 3: 19 and Deuteronomy 8:18.
- Remember that the Holy Spirit is your teacher and your helper. When you step out or continue to fulfill your purpose you will be living beyond yourself. Whether it's for strength, courage, wisdom, knowledge, financial resources, people connections or all of the

above, ask God for the tools and trust that He will make sure they come to you or you will be at the right place at the right time.

- Stay proactive but know when to stop and rest so you can hear from God. It's very easy to begin to rely on self or vacillate back and forth, but stay connected to God at all times. Trust me, with His guidance everything will always work out better than you imagine even when the natural realm indicates otherwise.

- As daughters of God, we must be encouraged by the fact that while we live and operate in the earthly realm, all our help comes from the spiritual realm. This is why it is important to be rooted like a vine to Word of God so you won't become easily discouraged.

- With your special and unique purpose in life you will be supported at all times by others who God positions, and by God Himself. Be realistic yet fully trust and expect your needs to always be met to fulfill your purpose.

- Commit to giving 10% of all income, from all sources, no matter what.

- Go for your purpose (don't procrastinate). A quote hangs on my office wall that reads, "If you wait for perfect conditions, you will never get anything done." Ecclesiastes 11: 4 (LB)

- Choose to release and discard any beliefs, dogmas, attitudes and behaviors that are limiting you from receiving from God. You are worthy of success and fulfillment as you fulfill your purpose. Take the limits off your mind and think outside the box.

- Because you belong to God and were created and called for His purpose, remain humble and sensitive to the fact that it's not about you, it's about Him. Your life gives someone else the courage to step out and fulfill their purpose!

- Allow the process to happen organically. Each of our lives is different and as a result, it is best to not compare yourself, your resources or your gifts to other Christian leaders—or those in mainstream leadership positions.

- Always remember that God will never leave you or forsake you.

- Do not doubt. Just as the flowers are bursting forth from seeds planted earlier with no signs of when they will bloom, so it is with your dreams coming to life.

The biggest reward from living a life with a passionate purpose is the self evident experience of the fact that none of your pain is ever wasted in God's economy. None of it is pointless. Not one moment.

❧A Message for Your Moment❧

ANTHONY & CRYSTAL OBEY

Your Time is NOW!

It has been said that success equals preparation and opportunity. I have found in my life that when I focus on playing my part, God does sooner or later present opportunities that line up with the vision He originally gave me. The promises of God may take a long time to show up, but when they do, it's all worth while. When I finally receive the promise I look back and realize that if I hadn't learned all the survival skills, patience, work ethic, and other things, I wouldn't be able to handle the advancement. I've discovered that the preparation for the opportunity *is* the opportunity. It's somewhat vain to focus your life on one specific goal far off into the future; your time is now!

Anthony and I had a beautiful wedding day—still things went wrong. But instead of just looking at one day, we enjoyed a wedding season which gave us plenty of beautiful "wedding days" shopping for the perfect floral arrangement, the perfect cake, and so on. We enjoyed talking about our life together and going out house hunting. We enjoyed the process. The secret to a great future is hidden in a great *today*; we can control today, but can't do anything about the past or the future.

The process and the transformation of all things is the mechanism that generates those ceremonial, symbolic days of realized accomplishments in the future. A person can't cheat all through college and expect to be worthy of their diploma; they will cheat in the real world because they didn't learn how to become great during the *processing time* of college. We are deceived if we think that we are going to take the moral and spiritual low roads of life in an attempt to inherit the Promises of God. The process is what makes one worthy of the prize, not the actual prize. A person who gains the prize without the process always misuses the prize and loses it shortly. "Therefore take the talent from him, and give it to him who has ten talents. For to everyone who has, more will be given, and he will have abundance; but from him who does not have, even what he has will be taken away" (Matthew 25: 28-29).

Embrace the Process

The Chinese Christian Christiana Tsai suffered from a debilitating disease much of her life. In her book, *Queen of the Dark Chamber,* we find these words: "Once a great scholar in China said, 'A sage seeks opportunities in difficulties, and a fool finds difficulties in opportunities...' We are born to overcome difficulties through the power of the Holy Spirit." Christiana Tsai, *Queen of the Dark Chamber* (Chicago: Moody Press, 1953), 12.

Some people race through life, just living for grand moments. We can't get caught up in the magic formulas of the world. Too many people are waiting for their 'ship' to come in while only a hand full of people are treading water out to their ship! God has called us to be people who *do* what we dream instead of simply dream of doing. As authors and publishers, we share this truthful phrase in our office and with authors who struggle with procrastination. We say, "Writers write!" If you want to be an author, start writing. If you want to make a change, start moving towards your vision. Don't dream it to death, move it!

The children of Israel cried out and murmured to the Lord for having to endure the wilderness. They never progressed into the Promised Land because they failed to realize the power of the painful process called the *wilderness.* Indeed this wasteland has claimed the passions, dreams, ambitions, and talents of millions throughout time. Don't let the wasteland claim your inheritance, embrace the processing period of God and become the woman He wants you to be, for there is no *prize without the process.*

A knife in the hands of an adult can be used to slice the Thanksgiving turkey, can be used to carve a work of art, or it can be used to remove cancerous cells from a patient; but a knife in the hands of a baby can be disastrous. God will not allow us to use the great riches that we are entitled to until we learn to embrace His process and allow Him to transform us into mature and tempered reflections of Him. Remember this, **the process is priceless!**

Instead of running from the pain of His process, we must learn to drink from this bitter cup—the same cup that our Lord Jesus drank from

(Matthew 26: 39). That's why you need never concern yourself with someone duplicating your success or stealing your blessing; because real success costs more than most people are willing to pay. Embracing your cross is embracing the process that yields your promise. So hold on tight, no matter how much pain you endure.

BE the Woman You Dream of Being

"Catch us the foxes, the little foxes that spoil the vines, for our vines have tender grapes" (Song of Solomon 2: 15).

We can't expect to become honorable, loving, respected, and virtuous people if we don't strive to *be* the best we can today. If you've got a dream of being successful in your career or ministry then you've got to be successful with what you have today. The quality of our life today is the seed of our fruit tomorrow. All fruit produces after its kind, meaning I should only expect to get back what I give out.

What we *do* today not what we *dream*, determines what we get tomorrow. We cannot live sloppy Christian lives and expect God to bless us with the rewards of a mature Christian. If

> *What we do today not what we dream, determines what we get tomorrow.*

you plan on losing fifty pounds, become an exerciser, and progressively learn better techniques of exercising and building a nutritious lifestyle. Don't make outlandish goals that you can't reach just to give up in two weeks. Instead create a *habit* of exercising and progressively increase.

I know a woman who got her stomach stapled to help her lose weight. She went out and ate the same food she did before this major surgery and made her self sick many times, trying to put the food down. You can shell out money or look to others to bring your change in life but if you don't have the character and temperance to handle your blessing then you're going to ruin the opportunities that come your way. No one can help us change our own nature. That's why gamblers hit the jackpot and go broke again; they are gamblers! Whatever they intake just feeds the fire inside of them. It's not about external circumstances good or bad, it's the inward condition of a person that sets them free.

Don't expect to become a phenomenal woman while being jealous, a gossiper, a busy body, bitter, a liar, or a deceiver. It's not the biggies but the little *foxes* of our day to day lives that prevent us from moving to the next level. The little sins constantly eat away at the integrity, purity, and awesomeness of people who don't end up where they want to be.

"Two are better than one, because they have a good reward for their labor. For if they fall, one will lift up his companion. But woe to him who is alone when he falls, for he has no one to help him up" (Ecclesiastes 4: 9-10).

If you really want to live a great life and truly become Christ-like then you've got to be accountable for yourself. Anthony and I are not only lovers but we are exercise partners, business partners, spiritual partners, and life coaches to one another. We kick each other everyday about one thing or another, making sure that we live each day the best we can.

If you're married God wants you to become life partners with your husband. The first and greatest institution given to man is that of marriage (Genesis 2:24). If you're not married, or presently have a troubled married then look at the people or person who God has placed in your life who you know you can share your life with and be accountable to; maybe it's your mother, your sister, a lady friend from your bible study. Finally, God does bring us through times where it seems like no one is there for us, but in these times God gives us supernatural grace to walk in self control.

You've got to partner up with people in life who think the same, believe the same, and are trying to get to the same place. I'm not talking about finding your clone but someone with the same spirit of excellence, the same appetite for life, and the same fire as you. Anthony and I are totally different but we share the same fire, hunger and vision. Watch out for people who don't have the level of passion that you have; they may dull your senses.

Soar with the Eagles

Eagles sit at the very top of the food chain. As she matured she would have the capacity to soar high in the sky and build her nest high in the trees or mountains. She would possess the potential to capture prey up to four pounds and fly at speeds topping thirty miles an hour. But if she grew up with chickens she would walk like a chicken, flap her wings like a chicken, eat the garbage that a chicken eats. If you know you're an eagle, don't hang out with chickens, soar with eagles.

You become what you ingest. A person who eats lean, fresh, and organic foods that are nutritious is going to look visibly different than a person who eats fast-food three times a day. Don't be surprised if the junk food diet produces bad health conditions early in life. It's true that you are what you eat. "And do not be conformed to this world, but be transformed by the renewing of your mind, that you may prove what is the good and acceptable and perfect will of God" (Romans 12: 2). Conformation occurs by ingesting, digesting, and then incorporating the things of the world, but transformation comes by constantly replenishing and filling our mind with God's word.

God is focused on producing people who have pure hearts. He wants our heart's desire to be Him, just as His heart's desire is us. The problem is that we have two natures battling for first place within us; our spirit and our carnal nature.

Experience Heaven Here on Earth

Stop looking for magic pills to success; stop waiting for your ship to come in; stop trying to take short cuts to your dreams. Don't waste another precious moment waiting for your change to come. C.S. Lewis taught in his book, *The Screwtape Letters*, that the devil wants to get us to fantasize or worry a lot about our future and/or reminisce and regret our past because we are the closest to God when we focus on NOW. "The kingdom is not here or there, it's not in your past or off in your future; it's now. Now when He was asked by the Pharisees when the kingdom of God would come, He answered them and said, "The kingdom of God does not come with observation; nor will they say, 'See here!' or 'See there!' For indeed, the kingdom of God is within you" (Luke 17: 21).

God is right here with you in this moment. He is your Promise when you haven't received your promise. Simply *be* the woman that He's called you to be and trust Him to change your circumstances and bring you the blessings, success, and promises that He made to you. All you have is this moment to show God how much you love Him. Don't wait until tomorrow to start being great, Your Time is NOW!

LIFE IN
CHRIST

If you have decided to become a Christian, or would like to rededicate your life to Christ, don't wait!

Pray this Prayer Today

Lord God in heaven, I humbly come before You thanking You for loving me enough to die for my sins even before I knew I was a sinner. I now realize that I am a sinner. Lord, please forgive me for all of the sins I have committed against You. Please wash me with Your cleansing blood from all of my sins and unrighteousness. I ask that You please give me Your mind to think new thoughts with. Please give me a new heart that is completely focused on You and a new life that I can begin to live for You. I now live for You and You alone. You are my Lord and Savior Jesus, so please lead me from this point on through the rest of my life as a Christian. Thank You so much for leading me to this turning point in my life. This is the most important day of my life and I thank You for leading me to it! In Jesus Holy I pray, Amen.

You are now a Christian! You need to tell everybody you know that you are a Christian now and you aren't going to be involved in all the sinful things you once were involved in.

Understand that you are now at the beginning of a life long growing process. God will help you grow as a Christian until you physically die and He receives you in heaven. Live your life expecting to be made perfect and trying to become more like Jesus.

Remember that God doesn't keep His people from problems; instead He Refines us by Fire.

*If you have decided to give your life to Christ or to rededicate your life, please let us know. Visit our website for a **FREE Report on Your First Steps as a Christian.*** www.RefinedbyFireWomen.com

HAVE YOU BEEN

REFINED BY FIRE?

Do You Want to Publish Your Story?

We are currently accepting stories for future books that will encourage, inspire, and empower people to continue following God's leading through life's challenges. We publish work by Writers, Pastors, Leaders, and Speakers who have a desire to be published and would like to expand their ministry options through the written word. If you would like to be a part of a *Refined by Fire* book or know someone whom you believe should be, please contact us at www.GMApublishing.com or www.RefinedbyFireWomen.com.

We are looking for exciting, dramatic, true, and inspiring 2,000 words or less stories. Your story must be informational and inspirational, and give the reader hope that they can overcome their own personal situation. To be considered for publication, we need from you: a title for your story, a focus scripture, a 50 word or less biography, a life application question, and of course, the story. You may submit stories for multiple books. If you have a special project that you would like to do for your group please contact us for more information. We ask that you email all information to us or submit it through our website where you can check out specific books that we are working on at any time.

www.GMApublishing.com
www.RefinedbyFireWomen.com

Were You Touched By a Particular Story?

Please share with us how the stories in this book have touched your life. You can be a blessing to the contributing authors by letting them know how you have gone through the same struggle in the past, or how their story helped you get through a current struggle. Contact the author directly or send an email directly to GMA Publishing at our website.

CONTRIBUTORS

Connie L. Van Berkel: Connie Van Berkel, a vivacious vibrant speaker, is the author of *Choose High Road Victories*, an empathetic yet nuts-and-bolts Godly approach to professional success for the Christian woman. Connie is an ordained Elder in the Presbyterian Church, a Bethel Bible series teacher, wife, mother, long-time career woman and church volunteer. To contact Connie for speaking engagements or to order her book go to her website: www.connievanberkel.com or email her at connie@connievanberkel.com.

Paula Bond: God has blessed Paula Bond with an awesome professional life. She began as a high-fashion model in Europe, then back home as an on-air TV broadcaster with BET, NBC and more. Currently, Paula's non-profit, *LIFE SKILLS ACADEMY*, teaches personal, and business preparation skills to underserved youth and emancipated foster children. Additionally her production company, *FIRST OPTION ENTERTAINMENT*, creates innovative galas, award shows and concerts. God has truly blessed. Visit Paula at www.firstoptionentertainment.com or email paula@firstoptionentertainment.com.

Shelly Brown: Shelly Brown founded *A Woman's Calling*, a newsletter and speaking ministry that encourages women all over the US. She has been married fifteen years to business owner, Carl Brown. They have three children, Jordan 14, Jake 12, and Delaney 10. Shelly has served faithfully at Orlando Baptist Church for 27 years. To contact Shelly for speaking engagements email her at sbrownocp@yahoo.com.

Nicole Cleveland: Nicole Cleveland resides in Norfolk, Virginia with her husband and three children. By profession, Nicole is a Fundraiser & Development Manager for her local Public Broadcasting Station. She is founder of Breathe Again Magazine, an online magazine designed to encourage, uplift and inspire women all across the globe. Nicole is also a television personality, hosting a weekly public affairs program on TBN. She is affiliated with many boards and advisory groups. But one affiliation means more to her than any other, and that is her affiliation with God. Visit her website at www.breatheagainmagazine.com or e-mail her at editor@breatheagain.org.

Sabrina Dubyak: A native of Wilmington, N.C., Sabrina grew up in a home plagued by violence and her father's alcohol addiction. Receiving Christ at age, 14 she quickly became active in the church. Sabrina began modeling and pageants as a teenager and had the opportunity to travel throughout the U.S., Europe and Asia; winning several local and national titles and the coveted title of Mrs. U.S. Globe. She also represented our country in the international Mrs. Globe competition in Riga, Latvia placing 3 rd in the world. The sudden loss of her husband at age 32 sent her life into a tail spin. Accomplishment and adversity have both helped to motivate her to share her story of perseverance through the valleys in life to again find the mountains that God wants us to experience. An animal lover and avid motorcycle enthusiast, Sabrina shares her story with a sense of humor and a humble heart. Contact Sabrina by Phone: (678) 779-2591 Address: 305 Westbriar Way Woodstock, GA 30189

Donna Dyson: Minister Donna R. Lee-Dyson served as the Maryland State and District of Columbia President of Women N Power International Ministries. She is the leader and founder of *A Servant's Heart Ministries* (ASH), reaching out to all women regardless of where they may find themselves. A focal part of ASH Ministries helps mothers of children with disabilities. God has anointed Donna to walk alongside women who have given birth to precious jewels that the world would otherwise cast aside. Currently, Donna serves under the dynamic leadership of Bishop Dwayne C. Debnam at Morning Star Baptist Church in Catonsville, Maryland. Donna can be reached for speaking engagements, prayer requests, or testimonies via email at minista2u@aol.com or at her website www.a-servantsheart.org

Valarie Fish: Pastor's wife, mother, writer, speaker, encourager; Valarie Fish is all these and usually in that order. She writes an inspirational column for her local paper, the (Magnolia, AR) Banner News and also one for the Baptist Trumpet. Valarie writes youth curriculum for Disciple Guide Publishing as well. It is her passion to point women to the Word as the ultimate life preserver in any sea. You can contact Valarie through her web site www.valariefish.com or by mail at PO Box 66, Emerson, AR 71740.

Nancy Kay Grace: Nancy Kay Grace is a speaker and writer desiring to share a touch of God's grace with women. She is married to her best friend, Rick, who is a pastor. They have served in church ministry together for over 30 years, and have had the opportunity to share Christ's love in England, Russia, Taiwan and Malaysia. The couple resides in Springdale, AR. They have 2 grown children. To contact Nancy for speaking engagements, please visit www.nancygrace.com.

Doreen Hanna: Doreen Hanna is a motivational speaker, author and founder of Treasured Celebrations Ministries. Her passion is to encourage women of all ages to discover how to celebrate in every season of life. Doreen & her husband live in Santa Fe, NM. They have 2 daughters and 2 granddaughters. Contact Doreen Hanna at www.doreenhanna.org.

Marilyn C. Hilton: Author and speaker Marilyn C. Hilton has written numerous articles for women and parents, and two books for preteen girls, *The Christian Girl's Guide to Your Mom* and *It's All About Dad & Me*. She and her family live in Northern California, where Marilyn serves as a church youth leader. Marilyn loves to hear from readers and can be reached by email at marilyn@rivergem.com.

Karen Hudson: Karen Hudson was born in Denver, Colorado and now resides in Evansville, Indiana, where she raised her son who is now 24 years old. She is a Communications Specialist for a division of Bristol-Myers Squibb. Karen is sharing her story of dealing with breast cancer and her renewed faith in God. She loves music, reading, travel, and the company of family and friends. Contact Karen at karen.hudson@bms.com

Feona Sharhran Huff: Feona Sharhran Huff is the Founder and CEO of Powerhouse Media Group, publisher of Solo Mommy Magazine (www.solomommy.com) and Black Boy Magazine (www.blackboymagazine.com). She is a regular contributor to Black Enterprise and has been featured in The New York Times, The New York Daily News, ePregnancy, Upscale, Ebony, and WWRL 1600 AM. She is a member of Delta Sigma Theta Sorority, Inc., New York Association of Black Journalists, Phenomenal Women Empowerment Alliance, LLC, and Downtown Women's Club. Ms. Huff is a proud mommy to Clara Caasi Sharhran Huff and Timothy Isaac Lewis Huff. Contact Feona at 718-425-9092.

Trish Jones: Trish Jones, a marketing mentor, inspirational speaker and business consultant, is the founder of Women of Influence Ministries, dedicated to taking God's purpose and perspective to women around the Globe. Trish and her husband, Chris, earned their MBA at the University of the West of England just months before becoming the proud parents of Elodie Christina. Visit Trish at www.womenofinfluence.com, email trish@womenofinfluence.com, or phone/fax at +44 117 902 9533.

Tammie Judd: Tammie Judd is homemaker and mother of five. She is a high school teacher at Peoria Christian School in Peoria, IL. Tammie and her husband, Eric, have been involved in church ministries for over 20 years. She and Jill Arnold (truthandlightministry.org) speak to ladies' groups throughout the country.

Pamela Kennebrew: Pamela Kennebrew is a Life Coach, talk show host, Bible teacher, and sought after conference speaker, and entrepreneur. She is committed to helping others live in victory through practical application of spiritual principles. She is President/CEO of Kennebrew Integrated Success Seminars (KISS) and Fit For Fifty. She and her husband, renowned musician and songwriter Rick Kennebrew are founders of Esteem Ministries International. As a professional educator, Pamela has traveled throughout the world. She is responsible for teaching/training international pastors and leaders from around the world. For more information please visit www.pamelakennebrew.com or www.esteem-ministries.com.

Christine Kumbin: Christine Kumbin hails from Nigeria with an unrivalled experience as a High School principal, college and university lecturer, crusade director and ordained minister. A prophetic prayer warrior, strong in faith and spirit, she longs for the lost, hurting and needy to be released from poverty into the glorious riches that God has purposed for them. Christine is currently a Pastor at the Elim @ Bristol City Church in England.

LaKeisha A Moore: LaKeisha A Moore is an up and coming writer with aspirations for national impact through motivational literature. A shy "country girl" from Louisiana, LaKeisha found her literary voice through composition essays in elementary school and, still today, continues to exercise this God-given gift through skits, poems, and inspirational pieces. You can reach LaKeisha by phone at 504-251-9841 or email at godspenmoore@hotmail.com.

Nicolla Renee': Nicolla Renee' is the Founder and Publisher of Inspired Living Magazine, a national publication providing resources that empower women to live God's best for their lives. She is a media and marketing specialist with a corporate background in television, advertising sales and promotions. She is a nationally published columnist who conducts business and ministry seminars across the country. As an entrepreneur, speaker and consultant, Nicolla specializes in helping women and entrepreneurs realize their dreams and implement strategies for achieving unparalleled business success by tapping into spiritual principles which help them fulfill their God-given purpose. Email: nicolla@inspiredlivingmag.com Web: www.inspiredlivingmag.com

Prophetess Thomasine Pickens: Prophetess Thomasine Pickens is the Pastor of Real Word Ministries, Inc. in San Antonio, Texas. She is a woman who has gone through the challenges of life and overcame! She has a humorous side to her preaching and believes that "life is serious enough....it's now time to laugh at your past mistakes and jump for joy towards your future." Thomasine travels within the United States teaching others how to TRUST in Jesus Christ. She has a weekly prayer line for women and men. She resides in San Antonio with her three "Anointed Warriors" for Christ! If you would like to schedule Prophetess Pickens to speak at your next event, please contact her at www.realwordministries.org, email to realwordministries@yahoo.com, or phone 210-363-5608.

Rebekah L. Pierce: Rebekah L. Pierce BA, MA, is the Editor in Chief of Average Girl Magazine (AVG), a motivational and inspirational magazine for women in search of change, purpose and prosperity. Mrs. Pierce is also a playwright, radio talk show host, motivational speaker, teacher, wife and mother. You can contact Rebekah by phone at (804) 274-8976, or email editor@averagegirlmagazine.com, or write to P.O. Box 4971 Midlothian, VA 23112.

Sauni Rinehart: Sauni Rinehart is a dynamic speaker, vocalist, and writer whose passion is to equip and encourage women to grow in their relationship with the Lord Jesus Christ. Founder of Triple-E Ministries, she desires to be used by God to positively impact lives in everything she does. Go to www.saunirinehart.com to learn more about Sauni's ministry.

Crissy Sanders: Crissy Sanders is a highly celebrated national speaker through Crissy Sanders Ministries. She ministers at churches, conferences, and retreats nation-wide bringing empowerment and enlightenment to a wide range of audiences. Crissy and her husband Dennis co-pastor Terre Haute Church of God in Terre Haute, IN, which is a thriving ministry that's received many rewards for its effectiveness to its community. The couple has one child appropriately named Joshua Caleb. Go to www.crissysanders.org to book her for speaking and to purchase her book or call 812-235-4324. You can mail the church at 2501 Thompson Street, Terre Haute, IN 47802.

Theresa Vogel: Theresa Vogel is an inspirational speaker and writer. She recently completed writing her first book, "Along Life's Path"—Inspirational Poems, Songs, and Stories. From the beginning of her life, Theresa has had many challenges. She was born with significant physical "brokenness" – resulting in burdens that would have held back most people. She faces life with faith in Jesus, and a "CAN DO" attitude. Theresa's desire is to encourage your heart, strengthen your faith, and tickle your funny bone. Contact Theresa for a speaking engagement at www.lifestapestry.com, or email her at lifestapestry2@yahoo.com.

Pamela Waugh: Author Pamela Waugh currently lives in South Bloomfield, Ohio. Founder of In God's Arms Ministries, and author of "In God's Arms" her years of experience with the hurting is where her heart has always been. Her ministry challenges others to pursue excellence in their walk with Christ. Learn more about Pam at www.ingodsarmsministries.com.

Marina Woods: Marina Woods is the principal of www.iMarketingPR.com, an internet development and marketing consultancy, and founder and editor-in-chief of www.goodgirlbookclubonline.com. Her greatest passion is giving herself in unconditional service.

ABOUT
ANTHONY & CRYSTAL OBEY

Anthony and Crystal Obey are the owners of GMA Publishing providing book publishing and marketing services to Writers, Pastors, Leaders, and Speakers. Anthony and Crystal Obey are a married couple who are spreading the message of victory in Christ through the *Refined by Fire* Book Series.

Anthony is an ordained minister and uses his preaching and writing gifts with his wife, Crystal, who is the creative and business mind of the team, to empower people through books, speaking, and other communication tools to reach their God-given potential. Anthony and Crystal Obey also help motivated writers become published authors through GMA Publishing.

They are partnering with women internationally to create books that allow women to share inspirational stories about overcoming adversity through the power of God in a world of hurting women. These books are known as the Christian Women's Inspirational *Refined by Fire* book series. There is no other ministry similar to what this couple is creating and women of faith are raving about the hope, encouragement, and sense of identity they feel after reading the real stories in a *Refined by Fire* book.

Anthony earned a B.A degree in Pastoral Ministry with a concentration in Christian Leadership, while Crystal has earned a B.A. degree in Human Resource Management Development; both from Trinity College of the Bible and Theological Seminary.

Anthony & Crystal believe strongly in being life-long learners demonstrated by their constant research and industry training on topics including organizational development, relationship dynamics, health, fitness, and nutrition, publishing, as well as spiritual development.

If you would like to invite the Obeys to speak at your event or would like to contact them for interviews please contact them today and they will be happy to discuss it with you.

ABOUT
GMA PUBLISHING

GMA Publishing provides book publishing and marketing services to Writers, Pastors, Leaders, and Speakers.

You want to be a published author but you have no idea where to start? GMA Publishing Helps Self-Motivated Writers Become Self-Made, Successful Authors!

Our mission is to help writers take success into their own hands by providing them with the book publishing and marketing expertise needed to become self-published authors. We also provide the most powerful tools authors need to promote their book to their audience. With GMA you get a complete publishing package to make sure that you have everything you need to present your work to the world. We also have marketing tools available to help you reach your audience in an affordable, professional way. We can help you develop creative marketing strategies so you can sell more books and build your writing career.

GMA Publishing has helped authors all over the world realize their dream of publishing. We have worldwide distribution lines set up for you so your book can be ordered by anyone in the world and you don't have to worry about trying to ship books internationally. We have published over 100 books and are now offering book coaching and marketing services.

If you are interested in starting the exciting journey of becoming a published author then let us help you. We believe in empowering self published authors so they have the confidence and resources to succeed. We look forward to establishing a thriving publishing relationship with you.

There are 3 ways to get started with GMA:
- 1 Hour of Personal Book Coaching
- 1 Month Book Writing, Publishing, and Marketing Coaching
- Book Publishing in as little as 90 Days

Contact us today! This is a great opportunity for you.

Reserve Your Place or Learn More at www.GMApublishing.com

Printed in the United Kingdom
by Lightning Source UK Ltd.
121072UK00001B/408